SECOND EDITION

Student's Book

5

SUPER MINDS

Herbert Puchta · Peter Lewis-Jones · Günter Gerngross

CAMBRIDGE
UNIVERSITY PRESS

Map of the book

The Science lesson

Alex, Phoebe and Patrick are good friends. They all go to the same school. Today they are in a Science lesson. They are having problems doing an experiment. Their teacher, Mr Davis, isn't very happy.

1 001 **Listen and say the words. Check with your partner.**

1 goggles
2 shelf
3 apron
4 explosion
5 bubbles
6 liquid
7 instructions
8 test tube
9 powder
10 gloves

2 002 **Read, listen and answer the questions.**

1 How many spoons of blue powder did Patrick use?
2 How many spoons of blue powder did the instructions ask for?
3 What does Mr Davis ask Patrick to put on?
4 What does Mr Davis say about safety in the classroom?

3 **Choose a word. Draw it for your partner to guess.**

1 **Read the clue and tick ✓ the subjects.**

Alex, Patrick and Phoebe are sometimes in different classes. What lessons did they have yesterday afternoon?

Alex only had one subject.

Phoebe only had two lessons.

Alex, Phoebe and Patrick watched a film.

	Music	History	Science
Alex			
Patrick			
Phoebe			

The film was about life in Ancient Rome.

Patrick loved all three subjects.

Phoebe didn't sing a song and didn't listen to any music.

2 **Complete the sentences with words from Activity 1.**

1 We __________ six lessons yesterday.

2 In Geography, we __________ a film.

3 The film __________ about the world's oceans.

4 My friend Clara was ill, so she __________ watch the film.

3 003 **Watch, listen and say.**

Language focus

Listen friends, to what I say.

Yesterday **was** a perfect day.

I **got out** of bed at half past three.

I **saw** a chicken under the tree.

4 **Imagine that yesterday was your perfect day. Describe it to your partner.**

Yesterday was great. I got up at ten o'clock. I ate chocolate for breakfast and I watched three Spiderman films on TV. Then I …

1 004 **Listen and write the names. Then sing the song.**

1 This person is not very patient. ____________

2 This person went after Phoebe. ____________

3 This person is Phoebe's best friend. ____________

4 This person is never early. ____________

5 These people can go to the past and the future. ____________

Phoebe was the first one,
She didn't want to wait.
Now she's lost in time because
She stepped into that gate.

Alex followed Phoebe
Because he's her best mate.
Now he's lost in time because
He stepped into that gate.

Patrick was the last one,
But then, he's always late.
Now he's lost in time because
He stepped into that gate.

The Time Travellers,
They're lost in time,
They'll never come back
If they cross that line.

The Time Travellers,
Travelling so fast,
The past is the present,
And the future is the past.

Phonics

2 006 **Listen and say the dialogue.**

Sue Do you want to go
through the gate too?

Ben Let's follow the friends till
the story ends!

1 Read and choose the correct face for each of the children.

1 

Mum Did you have a good day at school today, Alex?
Alex It was OK.
Mum Just OK?
Alex Yes. It was just a normal day. Nothing special.

2 

Dad How was school today, Patrick?
Patrick It was the worst day ever.
Dad Why was it so bad?
Patrick Our football team lost 6–0 and I was the goalkeeper.

3 

Mum What did you do at school today, Phoebe?
Phoebe We talked about the Geography project, and guess what?
Mum What?
Phoebe I'm doing a project on Mexico! I'm so excited.

2 Put the words in the correct order.

1 you / at school / did / today / ? / do / What
2 today / ? / How / school / was
3 today / Did / have / you / ? / fun
4 it / was / Why / a / day / ? / bad

3 007 Watch, listen and say.

Language focus

How was your day, Leo?	No, I **didn't**, Mum.
Did you **have** fun?	I **had** none.

4 Imagine that yesterday was the worst day ever. Ask your partner about it.

The EXPLOSION

1 **Work in pairs. Look at the pictures and the title of the story.**

1 Write down words that come to your mind.

2 Try to make a story out of the words.

2 008 **Read and listen to the story to find out if it is similar to or different from your story.**

Alex read out the instructions for the next experiment. 'Add one spoon of yellow powder to the blue liquid,' he read. Phoebe followed the instruction. 'It's turned green!' she said. Patrick was not very impressed. 'Yellow and blue make green,' he said, 'everyone knows that!' 'Wait!' said Alex. 'There are more instructions. Now take some of the liquid and drop it on the brick.' Phoebe did this and the brick turned purple. 'Wow!' she said. 'That's amazing!' 'It's boring,' said Patrick. 'Can we do the next experiment?'

For the next experiment, Patrick read and Alex followed his instructions. He put two spoons of white powder and one spoon of red powder into a test tube. Then he added some pink liquid. It quickly turned orange. 'Now pour some of the orange liquid onto the brick,' said Patrick. Alex did this and amazingly the brick started to get bigger. 'Wow!' said Alex. 'That's fantastic!' Mr Davis came to look at their experiment. 'Good work,' he said, 'but don't forget to read the instructions carefully for your next experiment.' 'That wasn't very interesting,' said Patrick. 'Let's do the next one.'

'OK, it's your turn to do it,' said Phoebe. She read the instructions. 'OK, we need some blue powder, some green powder, some orange powder and some green liquid.' While Patrick was getting all the things together, he knocked over a small cup of water. The water went all over the instructions. 'Careful Patrick!' said Phoebe. 'Oh no! There's water on the instructions now and I can't read a thing.' 'Let's ask Mr Davis for some more instructions,' said Alex. 'Don't be silly,' said Patrick. 'I've got everything here. We just need to mix it together and put it on the brick.'

'But we don't know how many spoons of each powder we need,' said Alex. 'Don't worry,' said Patrick, 'let's experiment.' Patrick poured all the blue powder into the orange and green powder. Then he added all the green liquid. Suddenly there was a big explosion and a bright red flash. 'Wow!' said Patrick. 'Now that *was* amazing. I think I added a bit too much liquid,' he laughed. Alex and Phoebe didn't think it was funny.

'What's that?' said Alex. He was pointing to a strange, glowing light. It was yellow and it looked like a kind of gate. 'It's really strange!' said Phoebe. The children walked towards the light and stepped into it. They were gone in a flash.

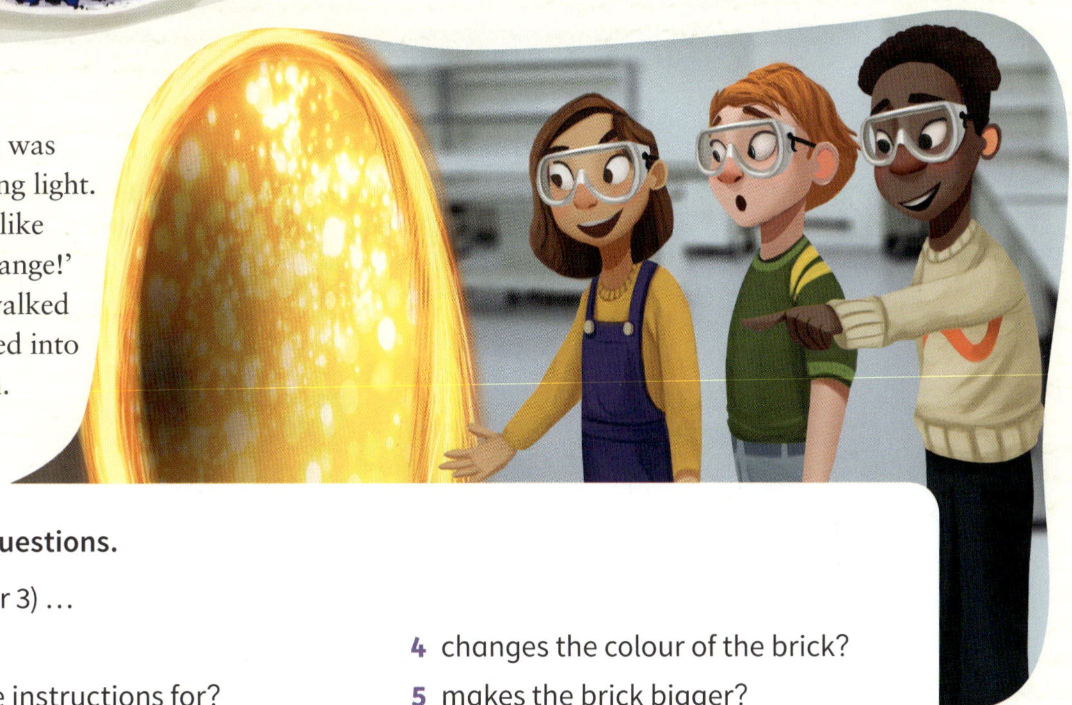

3 Read and answer the questions.

Which experiment (1, 2 or 3) …

1 does Alex do?
2 does Phoebe read the instructions for?
3 makes a yellow light?
4 changes the colour of the brick?
5 makes the brick bigger?
6 goes wrong?

4 What do you need for each experiment? Write *1st, 2nd* or *3rd* next to the pictures.

1 Disaster!

Pompeii was a city of 20,000 people in the south of Italy 2,000 years ago. It was a very modern city. Lots of the houses had running water. There was a busy marketplace, a theatre and there were lots of shops. The shopkeepers sold things that came on big ships from different countries around the world. The city was full of beautiful works of art.

1 009 **Listen and say the words. Check with your partner.**

1 smoke
2 volcano
3 temple
4 theatre
5 statue
6 columns
7 horse and cart
8 vase
9 servant
10 fountain

BIG QUESTION What are natural disasters?

2 010 **Read, listen and complete the sentences.**

1 The gate takes the children into the ________________.
2 Phoebe likes the gardens, the ________________ and the ________________.
3 There are no cars, only ________________ and ________________.
4 The mountain is not a mountain. It's a ________________.

3 **Choose a word. Mime it for your partner to guess.**

Look! Can you guess the word?

I'm not sure … Is it … ?

1 Read the article and write the names under the photos. There is one extra photo.

Earthquake shakes London

At 5.37 p.m. yesterday many Londoners suddenly felt the earth shake. We talked to some of them this morning to hear their stories.

'My sons and I were playing football,' said Ken Harmer from Wimbledon. 'We didn't feel much and we weren't worried.'

'I was in the living room,' said his wife, Claire. 'I was reading – it was strange!'

Their neighbour, Caroline, was sleeping when it happened. 'It was terrible. I was so scared!' she said.

Another man, Mr Williams, told us, 'When I felt the earthquake, I was standing on the balcony of our flat. It's on the 27th floor.

1  ________

2  ________

3  ________

4  ________

5  ________

2 Complete and say the sentences with the words in brackets.

1 At 5.37 p.m. yesterday, Mr Harmer and his sons football. (were playing)

2 Mr Williams on the balcony when the earthquake happened. (was standing)

3 011 Watch, listen and say.

Language focus

When the earthquake shook the tree,	When the earthquake shook the tree,
Leo **was reading** quietly.	The monkeys **were playing** hide and seek.

4 Ask and answer.

What were you doing yesterday at five o'clock?

I was …

1 012 Listen and correct the mistakes. Then sing the song.

I was sleeping in the garden, **(1)** ___________
When the ground began to shake,
A vase fell in the fountain. **(2)** ___________
The fountain fell in the lake.
I ran inside the shop, **(3)** ___________
And I thought, 'No, this is it!'
Yeah, I was feeling pretty angry when ...
(4) ___________
The earthquake hit.

Danger. Danger. Danger, everywhere.
Life is full of danger,
You'd better take care!

I was walking in the city, **(5)** ___________
When the day turned really grey.
I looked up at the clouds **(6)** ___________
And I knew I couldn't stay.
There was rain in the clouds, **(7)** ___________
There was smoke and thunder too.
I was feeling pretty happy when the ...
(8) ___________
Volcano blew.

All about music: PUNK ROCK

The first punk bands came from the USA and UK in the mid 1970s. Bands like The Ramones and The Clash wanted to change music forever. Their songs were fast, short and often very angry. Punk was about fashion too – scruffy torn clothes, amazing hair styles and lots of safety pins.

What I think about this song

It's great. It's OK. I don't really like it.

Phonics

2 014 Listen and say the dialogue.

Gran Your haircut is cute, Stan!
Stan I like your cap and cape, Gran!

1 Read Christopher's email to his friend. Some of the words were accidentally deleted. Look at the pictures and correct the email.

Hi Ryan,

Today we had a bad day at home!

Let me tell you all about it! While Dad was sleeping, the animals were very bad.

Our naughty cat was **(1)** __________ing our lunch and our dog was **(2)** __________ing birds in the garden! My sister and brother were even worse! My brother John was **(3)** __________ing my mobile phone and my baby sister was **(4)** __________ing on the walls.

I hope you had a better day!

Christopher

2 015 Watch, listen and say.

Language focus

While Leo **was looking** at the moon,
The explorer **was stealing** his favourite spoon.
While Leo **was swimming** in the lake,
The explorer **was eating** his chocolate cake.

3 Play the *wishidishing* game with a partner. Say a sentence. Your partner has to guess.

On Sunday afternoon, while I was playing computer games, my mum was *wishidishing*.

While you were playing computer games, your mum was reading.

No, she wasn't.

Was she sleeping?

No.

Was she listening to music?

Yes, she was!

A NARROW ESCAPE

1 **Go through the story quickly and find answers to the questions.**

1 Where are the kids? 2 What year is it?

2 016 **Read and listen to the story to check your answers.**

Phoebe started running down the stone stairs. 'Hey, wait!' Alex shouted. 'Where are you going?' 'Come quickly. Follow me!' Phoebe shouted. 'Why?' Alex and Patrick didn't understand what was happening. Phoebe was running through the city in the direction of the hills. Alex and Patrick followed her. They ran past the houses and the beautiful temples with their statues and columns, but Alex and Patrick didn't have time to look at any of that. They followed Phoebe up a hill outside the city.

When Phoebe reached the top of the hill, she sat down, and the boys sat down next to her. 'I don't understand!' said Patrick. 'What are we doing here?' Phoebe waited for her breathing to slow down. Then she began to speak. She looked worried. 'This city is Pompeii. We learned about it in History. That volcano over there is going to erupt, and we're in danger!' 'But how do you know it's going to erupt now?' asked Alex.

Suddenly there was a loud noise like thunder. The three friends looked up at the volcano. They were scared by what they saw. There was a lot of dark, grey smoke. 'I was right,' said Phoebe. 'We have to go and tell the people who live in Pompeii.' 'But are you certain it's going to erupt?' asked Alex. 'Look!' said Phoebe.' 'Animals often run away from natural disasters. We learned that at school. Now come on! The people are in danger.'

Back in the city, the children tried to tell everyone about the volcano, but the people didn't understand what they were saying and so they were not worried. Suddenly there was another loud explosion.

'Look!' shouted Phoebe. 'It's too late! It's erupting.' Everybody was very scared. The sky became really dark and smoke filled the air. Stones flew from the volcano and landed in the city. People started to run away shouting for help. The children didn't know what to do. Suddenly Alex saw a yellow light through the smoke. 'What's that? Look!' Phoebe and Patrick saw it too.

'I know what that is. It's the gate that brought us here!' Phoebe shouted. 'Let's go through it.' 'The gate?' Patrick didn't understand. 'Yes,' said Phoebe. 'Remember the lab? The yellow glow – the gate to the past. Maybe it'll take us back to our time. Let's run or we'll all die! It's our only chance!' The children ran as fast as they could to the light and jumped. They were gone in a flash!

On August 29th in 79 AD, Vesuvius erupted and destroyed the city of Pompeii. The volcano threw smoke and stones more than 30 kilometres high into the air. Within minutes, the stones, lava and ashes covered the whole city. Almost 20,000 people died.

3 Put the sentences in the correct order.

- ☐ They tried to warn people.
- ☐ They heard a loud noise.
- ☐ The children ran up a hill.
- ☐ Phoebe told the boys about Pompeii.
- ☐ Suddenly they saw a bright light!

4 Work in pairs. Read the sentences. Check the text and then replace the underlined words with more specific information.

1 <u>They</u> often run away from natural disasters.
2 <u>They</u>'re in danger.
3 … <u>they</u> were not worried.
4 <u>They</u> ran as fast as they could …

Let's find 'natural disasters' in the text.

Here it is. Let's look. OK. It says …

1 **Read this text from a website about disasters. Write *t* (true) or *f* (false).**

1 There are natural disasters all around the world. ☐
2 Scientists can stop weather disasters from happening. ☐
3 Scientists can always warn us about volcanoes, but not about earthquakes. ☐
4 Weather and people can cause forest fires. ☐
5 There can be a lot of damage after floods. ☐

flood

Being DISASTER SMART can save your life! Learn about natural disasters NOW

Natural disasters happen all over the world. We cannot stop them from happening. But we can learn what to do when a disaster happens.

The weather causes disasters like thunderstorms, floods, hurricanes and avalanches.

Scientists often know when weather disasters will happen. They give people warnings so they can prepare for these disasters.

Volcanoes and earthquakes are not caused by weather. Scientists have special equipment to watch volcanoes and earthquakes, but they often do not know when a volcano will erupt or an earthquake will happen. That's why volcanoes and earthquakes cause a lot of damage.

Forest fires can happen because of lightning, but sometimes they also happen when people are not careful enough and make a fire in very dry places.

Floods can be very expensive natural disasters because they cause a lot of damage. People should try not to build houses close to rivers because of the danger of floods.

avalanche

earthquake

forest fire

hurricane

2 **Work in groups. Think of a disaster you heard about. Use the questions to tell your classmates about it.**

Last year, there was an earthquake in …

- What disaster was it?
- When and where did it happen?
- What happened?
- What kind of damage was there?

1 017 **Listen to a news report about a fire and answer the questions.**

1 What day did the fire start?
2 How many helicopters are helping?
3 How can people help the fire fighters?

2 018 **Listen again and match the sentence halves.**

1 This is day five
2 Fire fighters think there is
3 More than 100 fire fighters
4 The biggest problem
5 Some people want to
6 These people

a no danger to houses.
b cause big problems for the fire fighters.
c see the fire.
d of the fire on Saddleworth Moor.
e are on the moors.
f is getting water to the fire.

3 **Think of a natural disaster (real or imaginary) and write a short report.**

- Think of a natural disaster you want to write a report about. Make notes about:
  - the type of disaster
  - where and when the disaster happens
  - what the disasters can do
- Read your notes to a partner. Make suggestions to help each other.
- Write your report.

This report is about forest fires. Forest fires often happen in the summer in countries which are hot and dry. Forest fires are dangerous. They can burn down trees and houses, and they can be dangerous for people too.

THE EARTH'S PLATES

What are the Earth's plates?

Super fact!

Plates can create mountains. This happens when two plates meet and the land on them moves up.

1 **Read the text and look at the pictures. How do plates make natural disasters happen?**

The Earth has seven big plates and some smaller plates. Land and oceans sit on the plates and the plates move very slowly. Some big plates can move about two centimetres each year.

The arrows ➜ on the map show where the plates are moving. The line around each plate is called a boundary.

There are different kinds of plates. Oceanic Plates are under the ocean. Continental Plates are under land. Some plates, like the South American Plate, are under land *and* oceans. The Pacific Plate is the biggest plate on Earth.

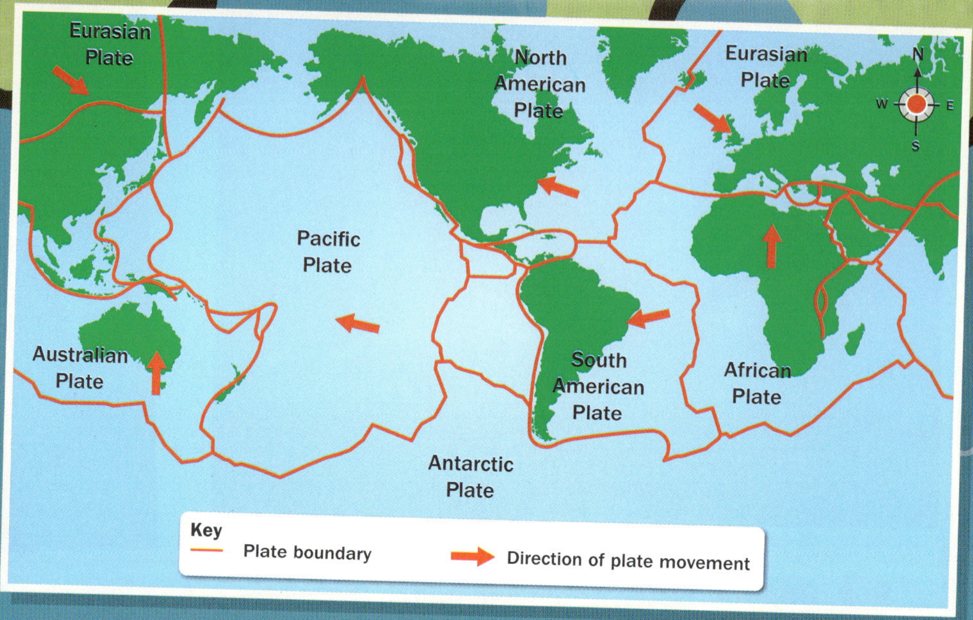

Where two plates meet, a volcano can erupt.

Where plates meet, an earthquake can happen.

2 **What are the words?**

1 These plates are under the ocean. ______

2 This is the line around each plate. ______

3 These plates are under land. ______

4 This plate is under land and water. ______

5 This is when fire comes from a volcano because two plates meet. ______

6 The is when land moves because two plates meet. ______

3 **Look at the map and at maps of your country. Find out:**

- which plate you are on
- the boundary nearest to where you live
- if there are mountains there
- if there are volcanoes there
- if any earthquakes happened there.

4 019 **Read this fact file about the Ring of Fire. Think and complete the text with words from the box. Listen and check.**

volcanoes	millions	452	cities	plate	earthquakes	40,000	water

THE RING of FIRE

- It's around the Pacific **(1)** __________.
- It's **(2)** __________ km long.
- There are **(3)** __________ volcanoes there.
- Most of the volcanoes are under **(4)** __________.
- About 90% of all **(5)** __________ happen in the Ring of Fire.
- Some famous and dangerous **(6)** __________ are Mount Fuji in Japan and Krakatoa in Indonesia.
- Popocatépetl volcano in Mexico is also dangerous because it is near two big **(7)** __________: Mexico City and Puebla.
- **(8)** __________ of people live near Popocatépetl.

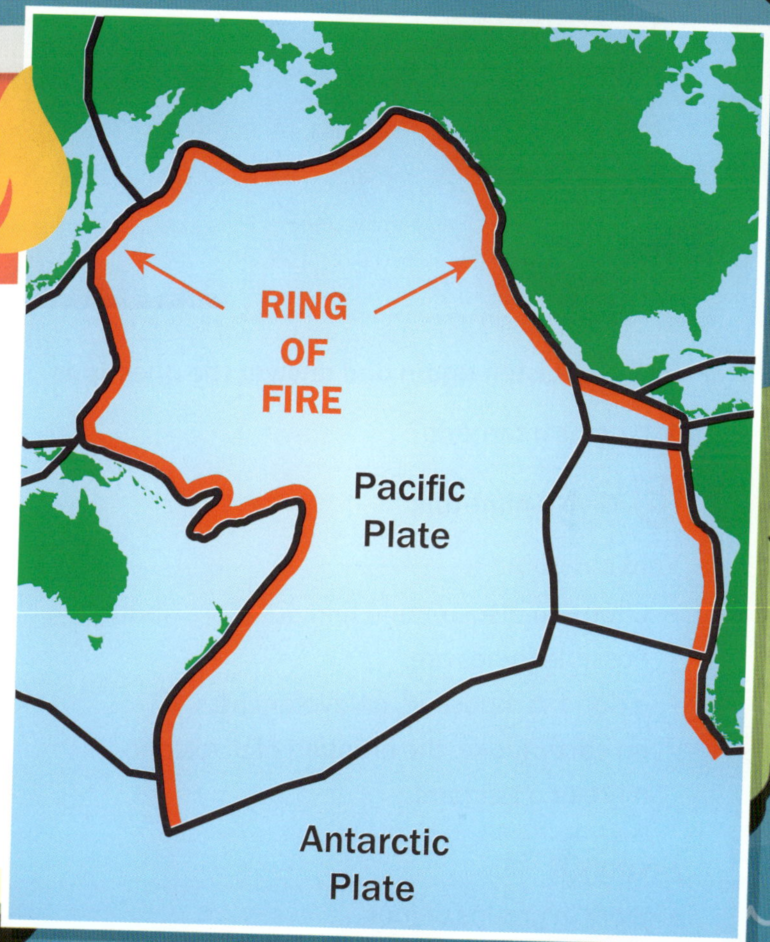

5 Project **Create another fact file about the South American Plate.**

- Find out about the South American Plate online.
- Look for information about how big it is, and about earthquakes, volcanoes and cities on the plate.
- Make notes.
- Design your fact file.
- Find a photo or draw a picture like this.
- Add a label for the picture.

Time to present

A mini-talk

1 020 **Listen to a group presentation about a tornado. Put the pictures in order. Find out about it.**

2 021 **Listen again and answer the questions.**

1 What is a tornado?

2 What happened to Joplin in the USA?

3 **Give a mini-talk.**

Find out about it

- Choose a disaster and find out more about it. Possible topics are: a flood, a mudslide, an avalanche, an earthquake, the eruption of a volcano, a fire or a tsunami.
- Use books and magazines.
- Talk to people in your family.
- Go online and see what you can find on the Internet.

Prepare it

- Work in groups of four.
- Find out some important facts about the disaster. Make notes on a big sheet of paper.
- Find four different pictures and print them out. Make sure the pictures or photos are big enough for your classmates to see from a distance.
- Write your talk. Each of you should write three or four sentences about your picture. Then show it to your teacher to help you with the language.
- Correct the text. Read it often enough so that you know what you are going to say.

Present it

- Tell your classmates about your topic.
- Point to your pictures while you are talking to make it more interesting.

A tornado is a very strong wind.

It destroyed lots of buildings.

The tornado in Joplin was in 2011.

Presenting tip

You should give a talk, and not read out your text. That's why you should prepare your presentation well, so you know what you are going to say. When you talk, look at your classmates. This makes your talk more interesting.

Think and write

Filling in a form

1 **Start a new portfolio for this year. Write about yourself in your profile.**

MY PORTFOLIO

My name:
Antulio Martinez

My class:
6e

My teacher's name:
Mrs Wilkins

What my friends like about me:
I am funny and good at singing.

What I did in my holidays:
I went to Lake Louise Summer Camp.

My favourite topics:
My favourite topics are rainforests and Geography!

What I like best about my English lessons:
I like singing songs in English best!

2 **In his holidays, Antulio went on a summer camp. Read the form and answer the questions below.**

1 What's his first name?
2 What's his last name?
3 When was he born?
4 What's his home address?
5 What country is he from?
6 What's his postal code?

Lake Louise Summer Camp

Last name: MAWNEZ
First name: ANTULIO
Nationality: MEXICAN
Sex: ☑ M ☐ F
Date of birth: 5 AUGUST 2013
Place of birth: MEXICO CITY
Passport no: TR 84902658
Home address (street): 1702, CALLE SAN JOSE
Town / Country: BUENA VISTA, MEXICO
Postal code: 37604

Writing tip

When you need to fill in a form, make sure you understand what you have to write. Sometimes you can guess what the words mean, but always check with someone just to make sure.

3 **In pairs, ask and answer questions. Then make a form for your partner. Check their answers.**

2 In the rainforest

1 Listen and say the words. Check with your partner. 022

1 beak
2 toucan
3 creeper
4 sloth
5 anaconda
6 branch
7 jaguar
8 anteater
9 beetle
10 pool

The Amazon rainforest is very large. It's called the Amazon because of the river that runs through it. The rainforest crosses nine South American countries: Brazil, Colombia, Peru, Venezuela, Ecuador, Bolivia, Guyana, French Guiana and Suriname. The biggest part of the Amazon rainforest is in Brazil.

BIG QUESTION Why is the rainforest important?

2 023 **Read, listen and answer the questions.**

1 What animals can the children see?
2 What's the difference between a tiger and a jaguar?
3 What do sloths eat?
4 Why does Phoebe tell Patrick not to touch the frog?

3 **Choose a word. Describe it for your partner to guess.**

It's a big cat that …

1 Read about the Amazon rainforest and match the numbers with the categories.

The Amazon rainforest is the largest rainforest on Earth. The biggest river in the rainforest is, of course, the Amazon. It runs more than 6,400 km from the Andes to the Atlantic Ocean. About 250,000 people live in the rainforest.

More than 40,000 plants grow in the Amazon including about 3,000 different kinds of fruit. The Amazon is full of animals. There are about 2,000 kinds of birds and mammals, 2,500 kinds of fish, 1,800 kinds of butterflies and about 200 kinds of mosquitoes.

1	six thousand four hundred	a	kinds of mosquitoes
2	two hundred and fifty thousand	b	plants
3	forty thousand	c	types of fruit
4	three thousand	d	people
5	one thousand eight hundred	e	km of the river
6	two hundred	f	types of butterflies

2 024 Watch, listen and say.

Language focus

100 – **one hundred** trees	10,000 – **ten thousand** trees
500 – **five hundred** trees	100,000 – **one hundred thousand** trees
1,000 – **one thousand** trees	1,000,000 – **one million** trees

3 Work with a partner. Write and say.

Two hundred thousand.

That's right!

1 **Look at the pictures and answer the question.**

Mia is playing a game. She's a monkey lost in the jungle. What do you think the monkey has to do?

2 025 **Read and listen to the dialogue to check your answer.**

Tom What are you playing?
Mia It's a new game called *Jungle Jim*.
Tom What do you have to do?
Mia Well, I'm Jim, a baby monkey. He's lost in the jungle and he wants to get home.
Tom Is that all?
Mia No. He has to find sloths and ask them for help.
Tom Is there anything else?
Mia Yes, he has to be careful of jaguars because they slow him down.
Tom Is that it?
Mia No, he has to eat bananas to give him energy. Do you want to have a go?
Tom Not really, thanks. I don't like bananas.

3 **Practise the dialogue in pairs.**

4 **Work in pairs to make your own dialogue.**

1 Choose one of these games with a friend:
The Magic Toucan *Jaguar!* *Simon the Sloth*
2 Decide what you have to do in the game.
3 Make a dialogue about the game.
4 Act out your dialogue to the class.

What to say

Asking for instructions
What do you have to do?
Is that all?
Is there anything else?
Is that it?

1 026 Listen and read the dialogue. Then tick ✓ the correct photos.

Guide OK, Mr Nelson, the tour starts at seven. So you have to be here at half past six. OK?

Mr Nelson Fine, what shall I wear, a T-shirt?

Guide No, no. There are lots of mosquitoes so you have to wear a shirt with long sleeves.

Mr Nelson Oh, that's right. I had to wear a shirt when I went on a jungle tour some time ago. Are my trainers all right?

Guide No, sorry. There are dangerous snakes around so you have to wear boots.

Mr Nelson Do I have to bring food and something to drink?

Guide You don't have to bring any food or water. We provide everything you need.

Mr Nelson That's great. Thanks.

a  ☐

b  ☐

c  ☐

d  ☐

e  ☐

2 Write the sentences and questions.

1 had to / You / sleeves / . / with / a shirt / wear / long

2 I / bring / have to / Do / food / ?

3 bring / You / water / . / have to / any / don't

3 027 Watch, listen and say.

Language focus

You **have to** wear a big shirt with long sleeves.
The jungle is dangerous, and so are its leaves.
When you walk through the jungle, do you **have to** wear a hat?
I **don't have to**, I'm a cool cat.

4 Write *yes* or *no*. Then talk about the rules at your home with your partner.

1 help in the kitchen ________

2 go shopping ________

3 take off your shoes in the house ________

4 make your bed ________

5 tidy up your room ________

6 wash the dishes ________

Do you have to help in the kitchen?

Yes, I do.

Do you have to go shopping?

No, I don't, but I like going shopping with my dad.

The PRESENT

1 Work in pairs. Look at the pictures and the title of the story.

1 Where are the children this time?

2 Who are they going to meet in the story?

2 028 Read and listen to the story to check your answers.

The children started walking through the rainforest looking for a way out. After half an hour, they came to a river. 'I'm very hungry,' said Alex. 'Me too,' Phoebe and Patrick answered. 'Let's follow the river, maybe we can find a village,' Alex said. The three friends walked along the river in the rainforest for an hour. They were hot and hungry.

Suddenly they heard a very loud animal noise. 'That must be a jaguar,' Patrick shouted. 'Let's climb that big tree over there to hide.' They ran to the tree and started climbing. To their surprise, the terrible noise got louder and louder until it was right above their heads. They looked up into the tree and saw hairy black arms and a tail above them. 'It's a howler monkey,' Phoebe shouted. They all started to laugh. 'That was a scary ten minutes!'

The children climbed down the tree and carried on walking for 20 minutes. Suddenly Patrick stopped. 'Look,' he whispered, 'there's a man with a spear.' 'We have to put our hands on our chest. That means we are friends,' Phoebe said. The man smiled and the three friends followed him. After 15 minutes, they saw some huts and a small village. In the middle, there was a fire with some women and small children sitting around it.

Two men appeared and they took the children to a very old man. 'I think that the old man is the chief, so we have to give him a present,' Phoebe said. Alex gave his penknife to the old man. The old man looked very happy and he pointed at the fire. The children went over and had some delicious food.

After dinner, a man took Phoebe, Alex and Patrick to a nearby waterfall. He pointed to the top of it and there they could see a yellow glow.

'We have to get there quickly or we'll never get back home!' Phoebe said. They smiled to say thank you to the man and started climbing. The problem was that the yellow gate was far out in the air. There was only one way to get to it. 'We have to swing through the gate on a creeper,' Patrick said. 'I can't do that,' Alex answered. 'I'm scared.' 'Follow me,' shouted Patrick. He grabbed a creeper, ran, swung through the air and disappeared through the yellow glow.

Phoebe looked at Alex. 'Let's go together,' Alex said. 'Quickly!' The two friends took the creeper, ran and jumped. They were gone in a flash.

3 **Read and tick ✓ the correct name.**

	Phoebe	Alex	Patrick
1 Who thought there was a jaguar?			
2 Who saw the man with the spear?			
3 Who gave the chief a present?			
4 Who was scared of jumping through the gate?			
5 Who helped Alex jump through the gate?			

4 **Read the story again and answer the question.**

How much time passed from the beginning of their adventure (when they started their walk through the rainforest) until they arrived in the village?

1 029 Listen and complete the trading cards.

KILLER CREATURES — Amazon series 2

THE GOLIATH BIRD-EATING SPIDER

WHERE:	In northern (1) ________________
SIZE:	(2) ________ cm
EATS:	(3) ________, small snakes, insects, (4) ________
LIVES FOR:	(5) ________ years (female only)

⚠ WARNING! This is a very dangerous spider!

KILLER CREATURES — Amazon series 2

THE JAGUAR

WHERE:	From (6) ________________ to Argentina.
SIZE:	(7) ________ cm
EATS:	deer, large (8) ________, (9) ________
LIVES FOR:	(10) ________ (in the wild)

⚠ WARNING! There are not many jaguars left. Humans should not kill them!

2 030 Listen again and answer the questions.

1. How long do male spiders live for?
2. What does the female spider do to males?
3. Where do most jaguars live?
4. How long can a jaguar live for in a zoo?

3 Use the trading card to write about the green anaconda.

4 Discuss in pairs.

1. Which of the creatures would you most like to see? Why?
2. Which would you not like to see? Why?

I'd like to see …

KILLER CREATURES — Amazon series 2

THE GREEN ANACONDA

WHERE:	Rivers in the Amazon rainforest
SIZE:	6m–9m
EATS:	Deer, crocodiles, turtles
LIVES FOR:	10 years

⚠ WARNING! This snake is not poisonous, but it is very strong. It can kill people!

1 **Read the magazine article and answer the questions.**

1 Were the men from the tribe happy to see the plane? Why (not)?
2 Were the scientists on the plane surprised to see the tribe? Why (not)?
3 Were the scientists on the plane happy to see the tribe? Why (not)?
4 Were the men from the tribe surprised to see the plane? Why (not)?

THE HIDDEN TRIBE

A few years ago, a small plane was flying over the Amazon jungle between Brazil and Peru when the pilot saw some huts. A few seconds later, the passengers looked down and saw men painted in red pointing bows and arrows at them. They took some photos and flew away quickly. The scientists were there to find this lost tribe because they wanted to show it to the world and show how important it is to make sure they have a safe place to live.

There are about 100 tribes living in the world that have never met people from outside. More than half of them live in Brazil and Peru. They live a life without mobile phones, cars and the Internet. They have no electricity. It's no surprise that they were scared of the plane.

Now many of these tribes are in danger. The forest where they live is disappearing because people are cutting down the trees to sell the wood and make land for farms. Another big problem for these people are illnesses. Their bodies cannot protect themselves against many illnesses. This means that when they meet people from the outside world they have to be very careful so they do not get ill.

2 **Imagine you are the chief of the tribe. Answer the questions from a journalist.**

1 Why are you scared of me?
2 Do you want something from me?
3 Is your life better than mine?

3 **In groups, present your ideas to the rest of the class.**

I'm scared because …

Ecosystems

▶ What different ecosystems are there?

1 Look at the photos. What can you see?

2 Read the text. What are ecosystems?

The ocean, the desert and the rainforest are examples of ecosystems.

Living together

An ecosystem is where many different kinds of animals and plants live together. Plants and animals get food, water and shelter from their ecosystem. Plants give shelter to animals. Some animals (herbivores) eat plants and some animals (carnivores) eat other animals.

The rainforest is an important ecosystem. There are lots of birds, insects and other kinds of animals in it.

Climate

The climate of an ecosystem is important. It can be hot or cold, dry or wet. Rainforests are hot and wet with lots of rain. This means there is a lot of water for animals and plants.

Deserts are dry with very little rain. This means that plants and animals in the desert need to work hard to find water.

Desert plants often have thick stems and leaves. This means they can keep water inside them to live and grow.

3 Read and name the ecosystem.

1 hot	dry	sand	camels	______
2 cold	wet	sea	fish	______
3 hot	wet	trees	parrots	______

4 Which ecosystems are near you?

There's an ocean ecosystem and a city ecosystem near me.

Super fact!

There are ecosystems in towns and cities. Many plants and animals live in towns near roads, buildings and people. This is called a city ecosystem.

5 Read the notes. Match the ecosystems with the photographs.

Ecosystem	What's the climate like?	Which plants grow there?	Which animals live there?
Tundra	Very cold and windy. Not much rain, but snow and ice most of the year.	No trees, but there are often small plants. There are some flowers in the summer.	Bears, sheep, seals, foxes, birds and some insects.
Wetlands	Cold or hot. Can be wet all year or rainy and sunny. Lots of water.	Plants with long, strong roots sit on the water. Some trees grow in the water too.	Lots of fish, insects, snakes, frogs and water-birds – sometimes crocodiles too.
Grassland	Hot and dry for half the year, wet for half the year.	Lots of grass, but not many trees. Some trees have long roots to get water from far below the ground.	Lots of herbivores like giraffes, zebras and elephants. Carnivores, like lions and snakes.

a

b

c

6 Play *true or false* with a partner.

Grassland is always dry.

False. It's wet for half the year.

7 Project Choose an ecosystem and make a poster.

- Find out about the ecosystem online.
- Find photos and draw pictures of the plants, animals and climate.
- Label the plants, animals and climate.
- Ask another group to guess the ecosystem.

Get talking

At the pet shop

1 Work in pairs. Choose a role card.

Student A

You are the customer.

You want to buy an exotic pet – a snake, a tropical fish, a spider or a lizard. Think about the following:

- how much it costs
- if it's dangerous
- where to keep it and how much space the animal needs
- what to feed it and how often
- if you can play with it

Student B

You are the owner of a pet shop.

Someone is going to ask you questions about an exotic pet they want to buy. You tell the customer:

- how much it is
- if it's dangerous or not
- where they should keep it and how big the tank should be
- how often they should feed it and what they should feed it
- if it is safe to play with the pet

2 Act out your dialogue.

Student A

I'd like to buy …
How much … ?
Is it … ?
How big does the tank have to be?
What do I have to … ?
How often do I have to … ?
Is it safe to … ?

Student B

OK, what animal would you … ?
It's about … . It depends on the size.
Some are … others are …
The animal has to …
You have to …
They …

Think and write

A description

1 **Read Tim's message. Choose the best subject for the email.**

School! My place Friends and families My hobbies

To: claire@megamail.co.uk

Subject:

Hi Claire,

Thanks for your mail. You want to know about where I live? Well, it's a small village. Only 7,000 people live here, and it's in the middle of some beautiful hills. I like it because there's not too much traffic, and there are lovely places where my friends and I can play. There's a very nice river and we sometimes play in the woods. It's fun!

The next town is about 30 km away. It's much bigger and has got about 70,000 people.

It's great for shopping.

What's your home like?

Tim

2 **Find these words in Tim's email: *fun, beautiful, small, great, nice, lovely*. With a friend, read the email without these words. What does it sound like?**

3 **Choose five of the adjectives below to describe places in your town.**

quiet huge famous long noisy new tiny interesting unusual old

4 **Write an email to answer Tim. Use adjectives to describe your home.**

To:

Subject:

Hi Tim,

Thanks for your mail. I'm going to tell you about where I live …

Writing tip

When you describe something, adjectives help you to make your description better.

3 The rock 'n' roll show

In 1955, Elvis Presley was becoming a rock 'n' roll superstar. Many fans went to his shows. By 1956, he was the most popular singer in the USA and had his first number one hit record. He had more than 17 hits before he died in 1977. He still has a lot of fans today. For many people he will always be 'The King'.

1 031 **Listen and say the words. Check with your partner.**

1 spotlight
2 backing singers
3 1950s electric guitar
4 fans
5 dancer
6 bass guitar
7 drum kit
8 bodyguards
9 stage

BIG QUESTION **What was music like in the past?**

2 032 **Read, listen and complete the sentences.**

1 Patrick thinks they're in the ________________.
2 Patrick's ________________ is a fan of Elvis Presley.
3 Alex prefers ________________.
4 ________________ and ________________ like the music.

3 **Put the words from Activity 1 into three categories. Add two words of your own to each category.**

places	people	objects

1 033 Listen and read the interview. Write the months under the pictures.

Interviewer So Suzy, last year was a big year for you. What are your plans for this year?

Suzy Well, I'm making a new record at the moment and it's going to be in the shops in April.

Interviewer That's great news.

Suzy And then in May, I'm going to play some concerts with my band.

Interviewer Which countries are you going to visit?

Suzy We're going to play in the UK, France, Italy, Spain and some other European countries.

Interviewer Are you going to play in the USA?

Suzy No, we're not going to play there this year. But we have plans to visit next year.

Interviewer So, a new record, a European tour. Is that everything for the year?

Suzy Well, I'm going to have a holiday in October. A nice long holiday …

Interviewer I hope you enjoy it.

Suzy Thanks!

2 Complete and say the sentences with the correct form of *be going to* and the words in brackets.

1 The new record in the shops in April. (be)

2 In May, I some concerts with my band. (play)

3 034 Watch, listen and say.

Language focus

I'**m going to** play a trick on him.
I'**m going to** sit and wait.
Look, he'**s going to** take a swim,
Oh, yummy, this tastes great!

4 Play the pop stars game. Ask and answer questions.

- When / make / new album / ?
- What / call / it / ?
- When / play / show / ?
- Where / play / concerts / ?
- What / do / for the rest of the year / ?

1 035 Listen and write the missing words. Then sing the song.

I'm going to play a shiny **(1)** ___________,
I'm going to drive a big fast car,
I'm going to go far, yeah, really far,
Because, baby, baby, baby ...
I'm going to be a **(2)** ___________.

Everyone's going to be my **(3)** ___________,
Every woman, and child and man,
I'm going to do everything I can,
Because, baby, baby, baby ...
I've got a **(4)** ___________.

Rock, rock, rock with me,
Yeah, roll, roll, roll with me,
Rock, rock and you're going to see,
Just how big I'm going to be.

I'm going to shout. I'm going to
(5) ___________,
I'm going to do the dinga linga ling,
I'm going to win. Yeah, I'm going to win,
Because, baby, baby, baby ...
I'm going to be **(6)** ___________.

All about music: Rock 'n' Roll

Rock 'n' roll started in the USA in the early 1950s. It was the first type of music that was very popular with teenagers and many older people did not like it. They thought music and dancing was bad for young people. Some of the most famous rock and rollers were Chuck Berry, Jerry Lee Lewis and, of course, Elvis Presley.

What I think about this song

It's great. It's OK. I don't really like it.

Phonics

2 037 Listen and say the dialogue.

Rose Are you going to the rock 'n' roll show?

Tom I don't know, Rose. I prefer pop.

Rose But Tom! It's Joe and the Holey Socks!

Tom Well ... OK, why not?

1 Read and match the pictures with the clocks.

A DAY IN THE LIFE OF SUZY SLICK

ROCK 'N' ROLL'S NEWEST SUPERSTAR TELLS US HOW SHE SPENDS HER DAYS.

My alarm clock rings at twenty-five past nine, but I usually get up at half past. I'm so lazy! Then, at ten o'clock, I have a big breakfast of eggs, toast and fruit – the perfect start to the day. After breakfast, at about twenty to eleven, I go to my computer and read my emails. I get lots from my fans and I try to answer a few. Then I usually write my blog and go to the gym. At half past two, I make myself a salad. Then I sit down at my piano and write songs. At quarter past four, I stop for half an hour and watch my favourite TV show. I never miss it. At five o'clock, I visit my hairdresser. In the evenings, I sometimes stay at home and relax, or I go to parties with my friends. I never go to bed before midnight.

2 038 Watch, listen and say.

Language focus

It's **five past** seven. Time to get up, and go!

It's **five to** nine. I'm hungry as a hippo.

3 Play the time game.

It's twenty to three.

Sorry. That's wrong. No points.

ELVIS

1 **Go through the story quickly and find answers to the questions.**

1 Where do the children talk to Elvis?

2 Where do they have a meal with him?

2 039 **Read and listen to the story to check your answers.**

After the show, the singer and his band left the stage. 'Go on, Patrick,' said Alex. 'Ask him if he's Elvis.' 'Excuse me,' asked Patrick. 'Are you Elvis Presley, the king of rock 'n' roll?' The singer stopped. 'Yes, I am,' he said. He looked very happy. 'I knew it!' said Patrick. 'My grandma loves you.' 'Your grandma?' Elvis looked confused. 'How old is your grandma?' 'She's 70,' Patrick said, 'and she's got all of your CDs.' Now Elvis looked really confused. 'What's a CD?' he asked. 'Never mind,' said Patrick. 'I just wanted to tell you how much people love you.'

Elvis invited the kids to his dressing room. They asked him about being famous. He said that it wasn't always as fun as it looked. 'For example,' he said, 'how am I going to leave the theatre with all those fans waiting? They're going to try to follow me to my hotel.' The children listened. Even in the dressing room they could hear the fans. They were all shouting for Elvis. Alex looked around the room. 'I've got an idea,' he said. 'I'm going to need that long coat, those glasses and that wig. Now listen carefully. Here's the plan …'

Outside the back door there were hundreds of fans waiting. When they saw Elvis, they all screamed and ran towards him. Soon they were all around him, taking photos and trying to talk to him.

Suddenly Elvis took off his wig, glasses and coat. The fans were amazed! Elvis wasn't Elvis! He was Alex sitting on the shoulders of Patrick. 'Sorry fans!' Patrick shouted, 'Elvis wanted a bit of peace and quiet.' The two boys got into a car and drove away. Nobody followed them. At the same time, Elvis was walking out of the front of the theatre with Phoebe, but nobody saw them.

Back at the hotel, Elvis thanked the kids with a fantastic American meal of hot dogs, burgers, ice cream and milkshakes. Elvis was really funny and told them stories about being a rock 'n' roll star. They were having such a good time that Phoebe was sad when she noticed a familiar yellow glow. She turned to the boys who were laughing with Elvis. 'Sorry!' she said, 'but we have to go.' The boys were unhappy because they didn't really want to leave. Elvis watched as the children walked slowly towards the light. They turned to wave goodbye and then they were gone in a flash.

3 **Correct the mistakes in the sentences.**

1 Alex was the first to ask Elvis a question.
2 Patrick's mother is a fan of Elvis.
3 Elvis took the kids to a café to talk.
4 Alex used a wig, a coat and a pair of boots for his plan.
5 Patrick wore the wig and the glasses.
6 Phoebe and Elvis left from the back of the theatre.
7 The kids ate pizza and spaghetti with Elvis.
8 The children were happy to leave Elvis.

4 **Here are some Elvis songs that were big hits. Can you complete them with the words in the box?**

dog	It's	Blue	me	Let's

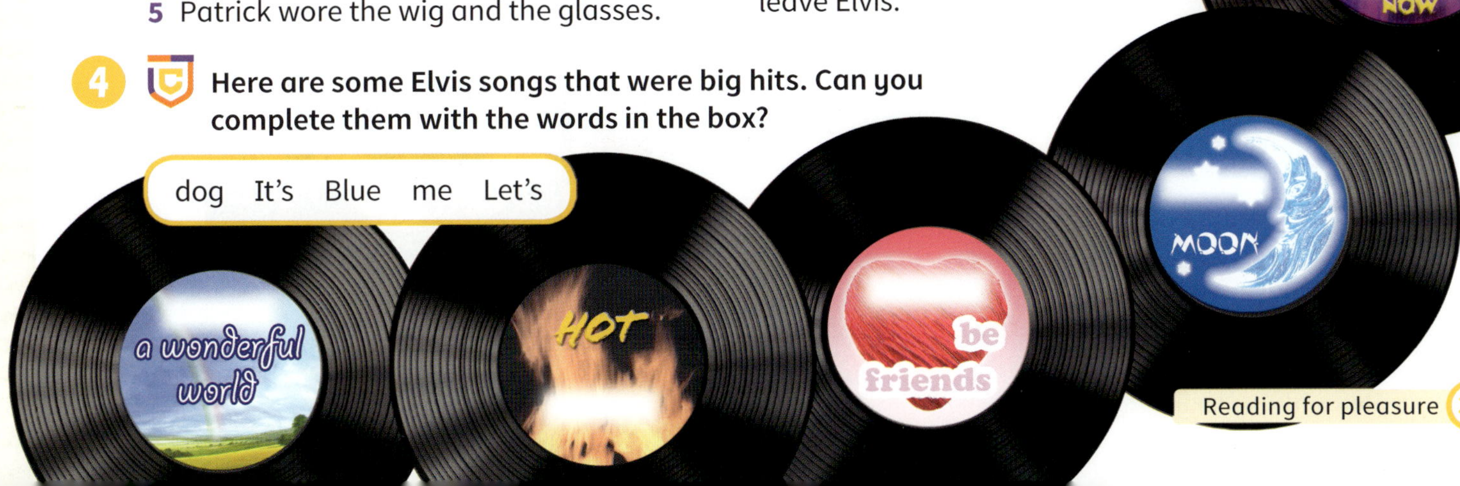

1 040 **Listen and choose the correct words.**

1 Buick / Chevy / Cadillac
2 Jive skirt / Swing skirt / Boogie skirt
3 Jukebox / Jivebox / Music box

1

2

2 041 **Listen again and answer the questions.**

1 When did factories start making the Cadillac Series 62?
2 How long was the car?
3 What did a lot of parents think of swing skirts?
4 How many records did a jukebox hold?
5 How did people work the jukebox?

3 **Discuss in pairs.**

1 What do you like best: the Cadillac, the swing skirt or the jukebox?
2 What do we have today instead of these three things?

3

1 Look at the pictures and read the posters. Answer the questions.

1 What is the girl with the guitar doing?
2 What do the boy and other girls think of her?
3 What do you think happens at the end of the story?

2 042 Read, listen and check your ideas.

Misha was very excited. She phoned Mike and asked him for a meeting. She was nervous as she walked into the room. The band looked like real rock stars. 'I'm looking for Mike,' Misha said. 'I've come here to play in his band.' 'I'm Mike,' said a man. 'Let's hear you play.' Misha started to play. After 20 seconds, Mike asked her to stop. 'You play well,' he said. 'But you're not loud enough. We're playing for Tony Parsons next week. I don't think he'll like your music.' Misha left. She was sad.

A few days later, Misha saw a poster. 'Backing singer wanted for Girlz.' A second chance! She phoned and arranged to meet Katia. She was nervous as she walked into the room. They looked like a real girl band. 'I'm looking for Katia,' Misha said. 'I've come to sing in her band.' 'Oh,' said the girl. 'I'm Katia.' 'Let me play you a song,' said Misha. After ten seconds, Katia didn't want to hear any more. 'You sing well,' she said. 'But you don't look right. We're singing for Tony Parsons next week.' Misha left. She wasn't happy.

Two weeks later, Misha was playing her guitar and singing in the town centre. She enjoyed playing for the shoppers. She looked up and saw a man watching her. When she finished, he came over to her. 'I'm Tony Parsons,' he said. 'I have a record company. I think you could be a star.' Misha was surprised. 'But, I'm too quiet to be a star.' 'No you're not,' Tonysaid. 'Lots of bands think that if they make a loud noise they're good. I saw *The Metal Kings* last week. They were loud, but they weren't good.' Misha was still surprised. 'But I don't look like a star.' 'You look perfect,' Tony said. 'Lots of bands think that if they look good then they're going to be famous. I saw *Girlz* last week. They looked good, but they couldn't sing.' 'But, but, but … ,' said Misha. 'But nothing,' said Tony. 'If you want to be a star, I can help you make it happen.'

3 Match the sentence halves to make the summary.

1 First, Misha sees an advert for
2 They are looking for
3 The band think she
4 Next, Misha sees an advert for
5 They are looking for
6 The girls think she
7 Misha meets Tony Parsons
8 Tony Parsons thinks Misha is

a a guitarist.
b a singer.
c doesn't look right.
d while she is playing the guitar.
e is too quiet.
f perfect!
g *The Metal Kings*.
h a band called *Girlz*.

MUSIC GENRES

What music genres are there?

1 043 **Listen and number the photos.**

rock music

hip hop

orchestral music

jazz

Super fact!

In hip hop, musicians don't sing, they talk over the music. These musicians are called *rappers*.

2 **Look at the table and read the sentences. Write *t* (true) or *f* (false).**

GENRE	WHEN	INSTRUMENTS	A FAMOUS MUSICIAN
Orchestral music	early 1700s–now	An orchestra. This is a large group of instruments including violins, flutes, harps, trumpets and cellos.	Wolfgang Amadeus Mozart
Jazz	early 1900s–now	saxophone, piano, trumpet, violin, guitar, drums	Nina Simone
Rock music	1950s–now	electric guitar, bass guitar, keyboard, drums, singers	Elvis Presley
Hip hop	1970s–now	rapper, electronic instruments	Missy Elliot

1 Orchestral music is older than rock music. ____
2 Jazz is less than 100 years old. ____
3 Elvis Presley was a famous rapper. ____
4 In hip hop and rock music there are often electric instruments. ____
5 You can only hear violins in orchestral music. ____
6 Hip hop is newer than jazz. ____

3 044 **Listen to four more pieces of music. Write the genres.**

1 ______ 2 ______ 3 ______ 4 ______

4 Read about Nina Simone and complete the fact file.

instrument where genre famous when sing

NAME: Nina Simone

(1) ____________ **BORN:** 21 February, 1933

(2) ____________ **BORN:** North Carolina, USA

(3) ____________ **:** Jazz **(4)** ____________ **:** Piano

DID SHE (5) ____________ **?:** Yes, she was a great singer.

(6) ____________ **RECORD:** *Little Girl Blue*, 1958

FAMOUS BECAUSE: She mixed jazz and other music genres.

FUN FACT: She started playing the piano when she was three.

5 Read and think. What music genres are popular today? What music genre do you like listening to?

What genre do you like listening to?

I like listening to orchestral music.

Popular music can be any genre of music that young people enjoy listening to and dancing to. In the past, it was often jazz or orchestral music. Today, popular music is often ________________ or ________________.

6 Project Make a fact file about a famous musician.

- Choose a musician.
- Find out about their life.
- Find out about their music.
- Find a photo.

Time to present

A show-and-tell

1 045 **Listen to Jasmine talking about her favourite singer and make notes.**

Jake Goodwin was born in ...

2 **What does Jasmine like about Jake Goodwin as well as his music?**

Jasmine likes …

3 **Take part in a show-and-tell.**

Find out about it

- Talk to your friends. Find out who their favourite singers or bands are.
- Listen to some of the songs they like.
- Choose a singer or band for your presentation.

Prepare it

- Find out more about the singer/group: name, country, language(s), hobbies, most successful song, how many songs, family … .
- Think about these questions and write down your answers:
  – Where do you listen to music – on the Internet, mobile phones, the radio?
  – Which songs do you like best? What do you like about them?
  – Collect some pictures from magazines or the Internet.

Present it

- You should talk for about a minute. Show the pictures. Think about questions you can ask your classmates.

Do you like … ?

Did you know that … ?

Presenting tip

If you want to use a difficult word in your talk, write it on the board before you start. Use the word in a sentence. Can your friends guess what it means?

Think and write

A diary

1 Read Jeremy's diary and put the paragraphs in the right order.

☐ Then, we rode to Whitewall Castle. There is a huge park with a little lake in the middle. We had a picnic.

☐ So we went home quickly. We were wet, but it was a wonderful day.

☐ Last Sunday, a group of friends and I went on a bike ride.

☐ Finally, we went to the stadium to see a football match. But the weather changed and it started to rain.

☐ First, we rode up into the hills near our town. It was great up there. The weather was beautiful.

2 Add these words to make Kylie's diary better.

first finally last Sunday then

SATURDAY 15th

Grandma and Grandpa came to visit me and my sister. We went to the fun park in Blackhill. Grandma went on the ghost train with us. That was fantastic. We walked to a very nice restaurant and had lunch there. I had chicken and chips, and my sister had a burger. We went to the town hall. There was a concert with Give It All. They are a new band from Liverpool. The concert was great. We were very tired and went home straight away. We went to bed at ten o'clock.

Writing tip

To say that something happened some time ago (last weekend, last summer, in 2011, three weeks ago …), use verbs in their past forms: *was/were … had … went … didn't like … stayed … loved.*

3 Think and write about something you did last weekend.

1 Write about it for five minutes. Just write, write, write. When you can't think of a word, make a line ______. You can add the word later.

2 Think how you can organise your ideas. Use the words from Activity 2 to do this.

3 Put your text in an envelope and seal it. Look at it again after three days and try to make it even better.

4 Space restaurant

1 **046** **Listen and say the words. Check with your partner.**

What will people eat in the year 3002? Nobody knows. Maybe they will eat pills when they are hungry. Red pills in the morning, blue pills at lunchtime and green pills in the evening. Maybe people on Earth will get all their food out of machines.

1 waiter
2 strawberries
3 biscuits
4 spoon
5 napkin
6 fork
7 knife
8 pepper
9 salt
10 chopsticks

BIG QUESTION **How is food prepared?**

2 **047** **Read, listen and answer the questions.**

1 When do they serve meals in the restaurant?
2 How is time different?
3 What is the date?
4 How old is Phoebe?

3 **Choose words and play the odd-one-out game with your partner.**

My words are *knife*, *salt* and *chopsticks*.

Salt is the odd one out. You don't use it to eat.

1 Read the email and complete the sentences.

Dear Megan,

Please tell me what to do. As you know my birthday is on the 3rd of April. It's a Monday this year. There's no way I can have a birthday party on a Monday. And I can't have the party on the 1st or the 2nd of April because I'm going away with my parents for the weekend. We're going to visit Grandma in Bristol. So what do you think? Shall I have the party on Saturday the 25th of March or shall I have it on the 8th of April? Please write soon.

Sarah

1 Sarah's birthday is on the __________ of __________.

2 She can't have her party on the __________ of __________ or the __________ of __________ because she's going away with her parents.

3 She can have her party on the __________ of __________ or the __________ of __________.

2 048 Watch, listen and say.

Language focus

This year the **1st (first)** of May is a Monday.

The **2nd (second)** of May is a Tuesday.

The **3rd (third)** of May is a Wednesday.

The **6th (sixth)** of May is my birthday!

3 Work with a partner. Ask and answer.

July

M	T	W	T	F	S	S
	1	2	3	4	5	6
7	8	9	10	11	12	13
14	15	16	17	18	19	20
21	22	23	24	25	26	27
28	29	30	31			

What day is the 11th of July?

Give me a minute. I think it's a Friday.

That's right.

4 Think of three questions to ask your partner.

When is your dad's birthday?

What is the last day of school this year?

My world: food

1 Look at the photos. What do you think Andy likes on his pizza?

2 049 Read and listen to the dialogue. Check your answers.

Mum Today's the 5th of December!
Andy Yes, it is. It's my birthday!
Mum Guess what I'm going to make tonight?
Andy What?
Mum Your favourite meal.
Andy Pizza! Cool! Cheese and tomato pizza with chocolate on the top?
Mum Yes. And there's more.
Andy Salt and pepper ice cream.
Mum That's right – just how you like it.
Andy Awesome!
Mum And that's not all. To drink – how about lemonade and milk?
Andy Lemonade and milk? I can't wait! What time are we going to eat?
Mum We? Well, I'm not really very hungry. It's all for you.

3 Practise the dialogue in pairs.

4 Work in pairs to make your own dialogue.

1 Think of a main course, a drink and a dessert to have with your meal.
2 Decide how to make each food funny.
3 Make a dialogue about the meal.
4 Act out your dialogue to the class.

What to say

Expressing excitement

What?	Awesome!
Cool!	I can't wait!

1 Read and correct the sentences below.

FOOD WILL NEVER BE THE SAME AGAIN

By our reporter Poppy Beanie

Yesterday, in his laboratory, Professor McKarrot showed us what our food will be like in the future.

Look at these two pills. 'If you put water on the green pill, you get broccoli with fish,' the professor said. The professor poured water on the green pill. But there was a problem. The fish was green too. The professor was not happy.

'If you put water on the pink pill, you get tomatoes with beef,' the professor said. Then he put water on the pink pill. The tomatoes looked like pink roses and the beef looked like pink paper. 'We're working on it,' the professor told us, 'We're not quite there.'

1 Poppy Beanie is a scientist.
2 Professor McKarrot showed her how to make food in the future.
3 If you put coffee on the green pill, you get broccoli with fish.
4 If you put water on the pink pill, you get tomatoes with chicken.

2 050 Watch, listen and say.

Language focus

If you **leave** chocolate in the sun, it quickly **melts**.

If you **put** honey in your tea, it **makes** it sweet.

3 Play the food game with a partner. Imagine that you have pills of six different colours. Tell your partner what food you get.

If you put water on the blue pill, you get potatoes with spinach.

1 **Look at the pictures. Where can you see these things?**

1 knives and forks
2 lots of washing up
3 a birthday cake
4 pots with steam

2 051 **Go through the text quickly. Why does the robot want the children to do the washing up? Listen and check your answer.**

The friends sat down at the table. After ten minutes, the waiter came with the starter. There were three bowls with something orange in them. 'Orange soup with fish and pepper,' the waiter said. They tried to eat the soup with their spoons, but it didn't work. The soup was hard. 'If you throw your soup into the air, you can eat it more easily,' said the waiter. So they threw the soup out of the bowls into the air. The soup fell onto the table and broke into hundreds of little orange balls. The children tried to pick up the balls with their spoons, but they always rolled away. 'It's easier if you use your chopsticks,' the waiter said. So they ate the little balls with their chopsticks. 'The soup is really good,' Phoebe said. 'It tastes like fishy, peppery sweets.' 'I like it too,' Alex agreed, 'but I'm still hungry.'

The waiter came in with the second course. There were four big pots with lids on. When the waiter took the lids off, coloured steam came out of them. 'Beef, carrots, broccoli and crocodile,' he said. 'You have to eat the steam fast or it will disappear.' The children took their spoons and tried to eat the steam as quickly as possible, but they didn't get much. 'I can't believe that all we have to eat is soup and steam!' said Alex. 'What's for dessert?' the children asked. 'Wait and see,' answered the waiter.

The kitchen door opened with a loud noise. Phoebe, Alex and Patrick saw a huge spaceship sailing towards them. On it there were lots and lots of burning candles. 'Happy birthday!' shouted the waiter as the spaceship landed in front of Phoebe.

'Blow out the candles,' Alex said. 'Please help me,' answered Phoebe, 'there are too many.' So, together they blew out the candles. 'Hurray, the spaceship is made of chocolate and there's ice cream inside,' Phoebe shouted. Alex, Patrick and Phoebe ate until they were full.

'That was wonderful,' Phoebe said. At that moment, the waiter came and gave them the bill. 'It's 60,000 goldstars altogether,' he said.

'What? We, we … haven't got any goldstars,' Patrick answered. The waiter scratched his head. 'Then I'm afraid that you have to work in the kitchen for a week.' The children nodded sadly and walked towards the kitchen. When they got to the door, a golden glow appeared around it. They looked at each other happily and walked into it. They were gone in a flash.

3 **Read and answer the questions.**

1 What was the first course?
2 How could they catch the orange balls?
3 What was the second course?
4 What did they have for dessert?
5 What money does the restaurant take?
6 What did the waiter tell them to do?

4 **Read and match the prices with the objects.**

If a three-course meal for three costs 60,000 goldstars, how much do you think these things cost at the edge of the universe?

1,000 goldstars   10,000 goldstars   50,000 goldstars   100,000 goldstars

1 

A can of space cola

2 
A trip to the 6D cinema

3 
A jet booster bike

4 
A pet zonk

1 **Read the blog and match the pictures with the paragraphs.**

FANTASTIC FOOD

My favourite book is *Charlie and the Chocolate Factory* by the wonderful Roald Dahl. The hero is a small boy called Charlie Bucket, but the real hero of the book is Willy Wonka. In his chocolate factory, he makes the most amazing sweets. Here are just a few of the most wonderful sweets he makes:

1 Chewing gum that is a complete meal: tomato soup followed by roast chicken, and then strawberries with cream. He also has a chewing gum that never loses its flavour.

2 Hot ice cream for a cold day! What a great idea. Now I can eat ice cream every day! He also has an ice cream that never melts.

3 Paper that you can lick. The paper comes with pictures of fruit all over it: oranges, grapes, apples, bananas. When you lick the pictures, you taste the fruit. Brilliant!

4 Lollipops with lights in them. They are perfect for eating in bed and reading at night.

5 Grass made of sugar, called swudge. It grows by the chocolate river and the chocolate waterfall in his factory.

6 He has some great sweets for schoolchildren, like invisible chocolate bars for eating in the classroom. The teacher can't tell you off for eating this because they can't see it. There are also sugar-coated pencils for sucking and magic hand-fudge – you hold the fudge in your hand and you taste it in your mouth.

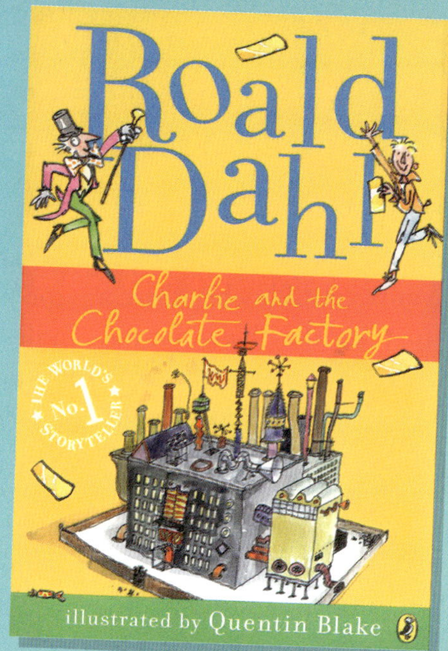

2 **Imagine you have a sweet factory. Discuss the questions.**

1 Which of the sweets would you like to make the most?

2 What three courses would your chewing gum be?

3 What flavours would you put on your paper?

HOW TO MAKE

hot chocolate swudge

STRAIGHT FROM

Willy Wonka's factory!

1 **Write the numbers under the photos.**

1 an ice-cream glass
2 an ice-cream scoop
3 a pan
4 a straw

You need:

 ______

 ______

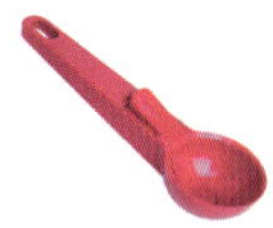 ______

 ______

2 052 **Listen and write the missing numbers.**

____ bottle(s) of chocolate sauce

____ bag(s) of green sweets

____ g of chocolate

____ ml of cream

____ spoons of sugar

____ balls of ice cream

3 053 **Listen and write in the ingredients.**

1 Take the glass and add some ______________.

2 Cut the ______________ to make grass.

3 Break the ______________ and melt it in a pan.

4 Add the sugar and the ______________.

5 Next, pour the mixture into the glass over the chocolate sauce. Then, add the ______________.

6 Finally, put the ______________ on top.

4 **Invent a delicious drink. Then present your drink to the class.**

It's called …

The ingredients are …

To make it, first … / Then, … / Finally, …

MAKING CHOCOLATE

How is chocolate made?

1 054 Listen and number the photos.

factory

pod

roast

chocolate paste

mould

cacao tree

2 Read about the start of making chocolate. Complete with the words from the box.

trees	lorries	pods
sun	cacao	seeds

It all starts in pods growing on a ___________ tree. Pods grow from the branches and stem of the cacao tree.

After some time, the ___________ are red, yellow or orange. Now they are ready for cutting.

Next, farm workers take the pods off the ___________ and open them. There are about 20 to 50 ___________ inside each pod. The seeds are called cacao beans. Workers cut them carefully out of the pods.

Workers leave the beans to dry in the ___________ or a special room for about a week. This makes the beans taste sweeter.

Finally, when the beans are dry, they go on ships or ___________ to chocolate factories.

3 What happens at the chocolate factory? Read and match the pictures with the sentences.

1	The beans are cleaned by factory workers.
2	The beans are roasted until the outside comes off.
3	The inside of the beans is made into chocolate paste.
4	Sugar, milk or butter is added to the chocolate paste.
5	The chocolate paste is put into moulds until it gets cold.

Super fact!

Chocolate is the only food that melts at just less than human body temperature. This is why chocolate melts in your mouth!

4 Project **Make a chart about the process of making jam in a factory.**

- Find out about the process online.
- Think about each step.
- Draw a picture for each step.
- Add a label for each step.
- Draw arrows showing the order of the steps.
- Describe the process to your class.

Get talking

At the restaurant

1 Work in pairs. Choose a role card.

Student A

You are the customer.

You are having a meal in a restaurant.
Think about the following:

- saying hello
- asking for the menu
- ordering a drink
- ordering starters
- ordering the main course
- ordering another drink
- ordering dessert
- asking for the bill
- saying goodbye

Student B

You are the waiter/waitress.

Think about the following:

- saying hello to the guest and showing them a table
- bringing the menu
- asking what they would like to drink
- asking what they would like to eat
- asking if they would like anything else
- asking if everything was all right
- bringing the bill
- saying thank you

2 Act out your dialogue.

Student A

Hello, have you got a table for … ?
I'd like to see …
What do you suggest?
For starters I'd like …
Then I'll have …
Can I have … with the … ?
Can I have another … ?
Could you please bring me … ?
Can I have … ?

Student B

Please follow me.
What would you like … ?
Can I suggest the … ?
The … is very good.
You certainly can.
Of course.
Is everything … ?
Here's the …

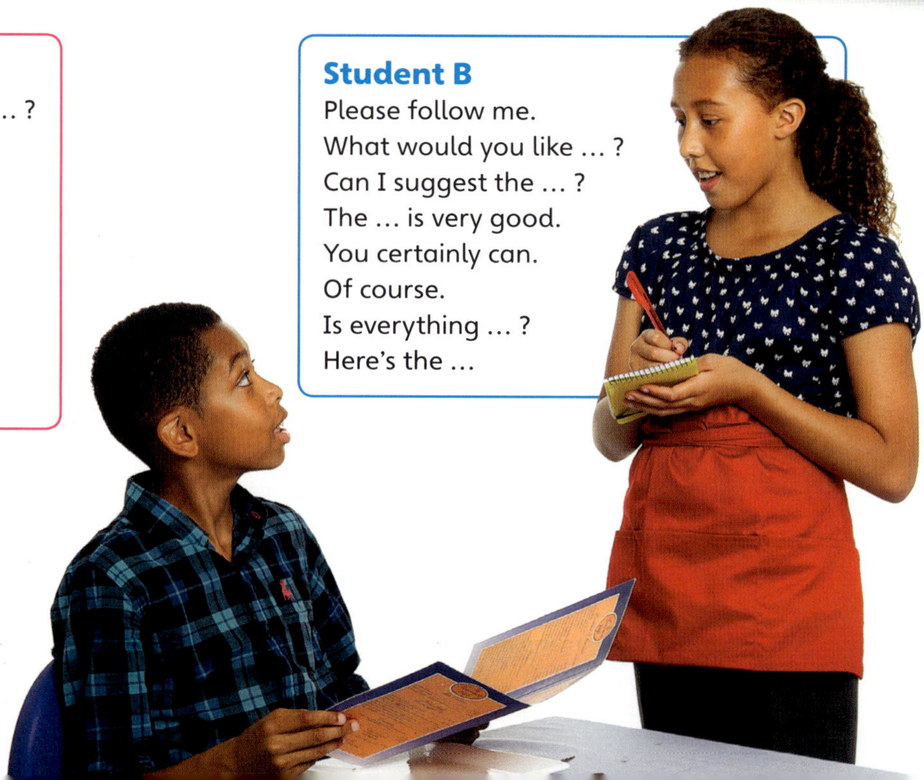

Think and write

A recipe

1 Read the recipe.

1 Complete the text with the phrases from the box.
2 Match the words (1–4) with the pictures.

Things you need Ingredients How to make it

Apple Surprise

Preparation time: 10 minutes

(1) ____________

2 small red apples
2 tbsp.*lemon juice
2 tbsp. sugar
a little bit of cinnamon
some vanilla ice cream

(2) ____________

1 knife 3 blender
2 a tablespoon 4 serving bowls

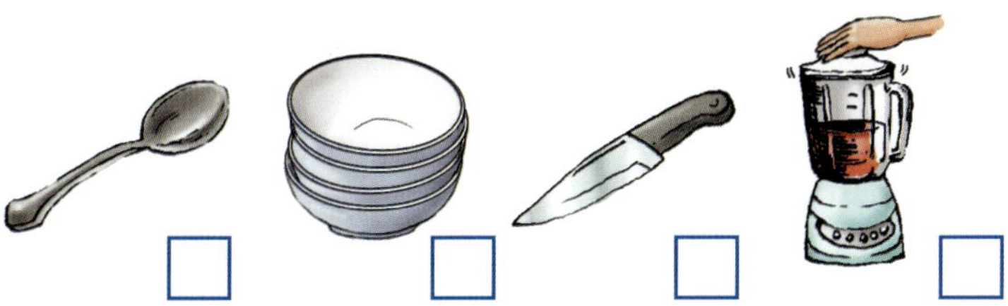

(3) ____________

- Peel the apples and cut them into small pieces. Throw away the core.
- Put the apple pieces and lemon juice into the blender. Blend until the mixture is very smooth.
- Pour the mixture into a small bowl and stir in the sugar and cinnamon.
- Pour over your ice cream and enjoy!

Note:
Use a knife only when a parent or another adult is present!

*tbsp. = tablespoon

2 Circle the verbs in the recipe and write them under the pictures.

1 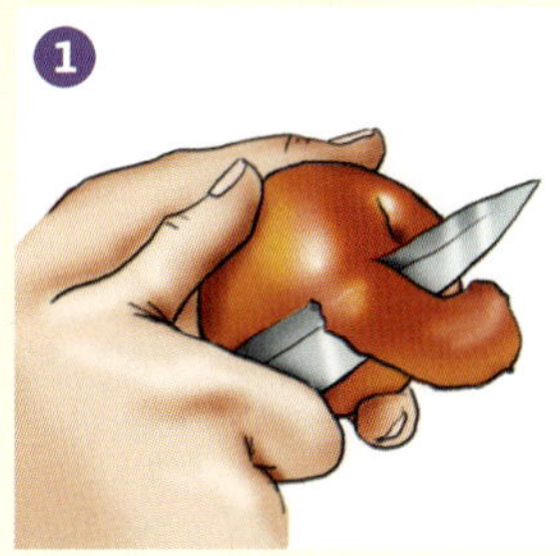
____

2 
____

3 
____

4 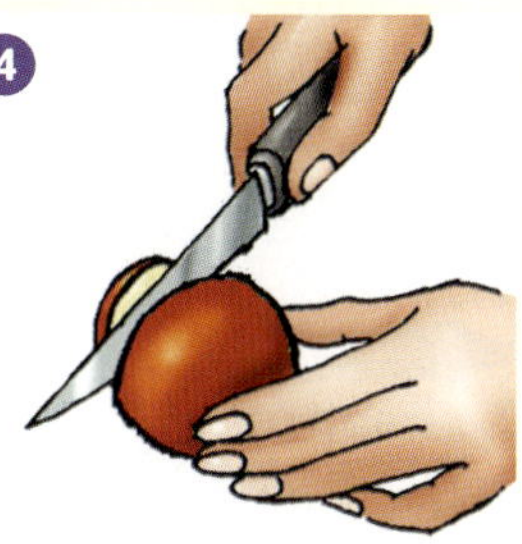
____

5 
____

3 Write your own recipe. Include information about *Ingredients*, *Time*, *Things you need*, *Preparation* and *How to make it*. Find a good name for your recipe.

Writing tip

When you create your own recipe, use verbs such as: *put in, stir, peel, cut, pour.*

Use the following language to say how much: *a little bit of, a tablespoon of, a cup of, half a litre of, half a kilo of.*

5 The Wild West

1 055 **Listen and say the words. Check with your partner.**

The Wild West describes part of North America in the second half of the 19th century. It was a time when people were travelling across North America, discovering new land and building new towns. It was also the time of cowboys, both good and bad!

1 robbers
2 jail
3 wagon
4 sheriff
5 saddle
6 pistol
7 handcuffs
8 rope
9 barrel

BIG QUESTION What was life like in the Wild West?

2 056 **Read, listen and complete the sentences.**

1 Patrick loves ________________.
2 Alex thinks the men on horses are ________________.
3 The sheriff is wearing a badge and has got a ________________ in his holster.
4 Phoebe thinks the sheriff looks ________________.

3 **Choose a word. Describe it for your partner to guess.**

You find this on a horse.

Is it a ... ?

1 Match the sentences with the pictures.

1 It's made of wood and metal.
2 It's made of cotton.
3 They're made of leather.
4 It's used for hiding your face.
5 They're made of glass.
6 They're used for keeping your feet warm.
7 They're used for holding water.
8 It's used for travelling to places.

2 Put the words in the correct order.

1 boots / made / are / The / leather / . / of
2 made / The / glass / . / is / of / bottle
3 your feet / used / for / warm / . / keeping / are / The boots
4 The / water / . / holding / for / used / bottle / is

3 057 Watch, listen and say.

Language focus

This cage **is made of** metal.
It**'s used for** catching me.
These boots **are made of** leather.
They**'re used for** drinking tea!

4 Play the guessing game.

I'm thinking of an object.

Is it made of wood?

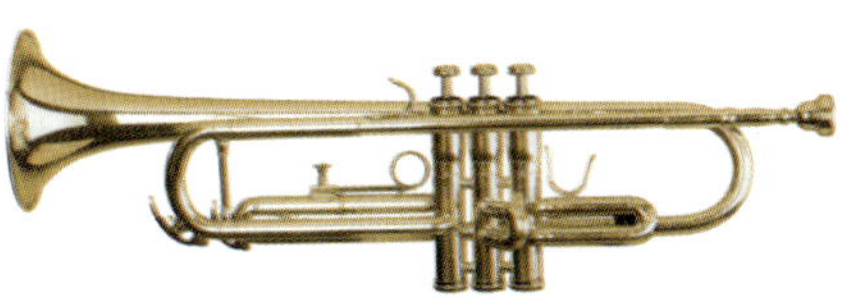

1 058 Listen and write the missing words. Then sing the song.

His gun was made of **(1)** ______________,
His teeth were black and **(2)** ______________.
His name was Billie Liar,
The meanest robber in town.

When Billie rode along the **(3)** ______________,
The people all got down,
And hid behind the **(4)** ______________,
From the meanest robber in town.

Billie robbed a lot of **(5)** ______________,
He went from town to town.
Not a single **(6)** ______________ was ever safe,
From the meanest robber in town.

One day he robbed a **(7)** ______________,
As it came into the town,
And that was the one **(8)** ______________,
From the meanest robber in town.

Sitting inside the stagecoach,
Dressed in **(9)** ______________ and brown,
Was **(10)** ______________ William Teller,
The quickest man in town.

The sheriff grabbed the robber,
And threw him to the ground.
Now Billie Liar's behind the bars
Of the safest **(11)** ______________ in town.

All about music:

COUNTRY AND WESTERN

Country and Western music came from the USA in the 1920s. The songs were often about cowboys and told stories of the early settlers. These days the music is still very popular in America and in many other parts of the world as well.

What I think about this song

- It's great.
- It's OK.
- I don't really like it.

Phonics

2 060 Listen and say the dialogue.

Eddie Run, Jenny! Billie's getting out his gun!

Jenny Well, I'm not running, Eddie. He's got a bubble gun!

1 **Follow the lines and write *t* (true) or *f* (false).**

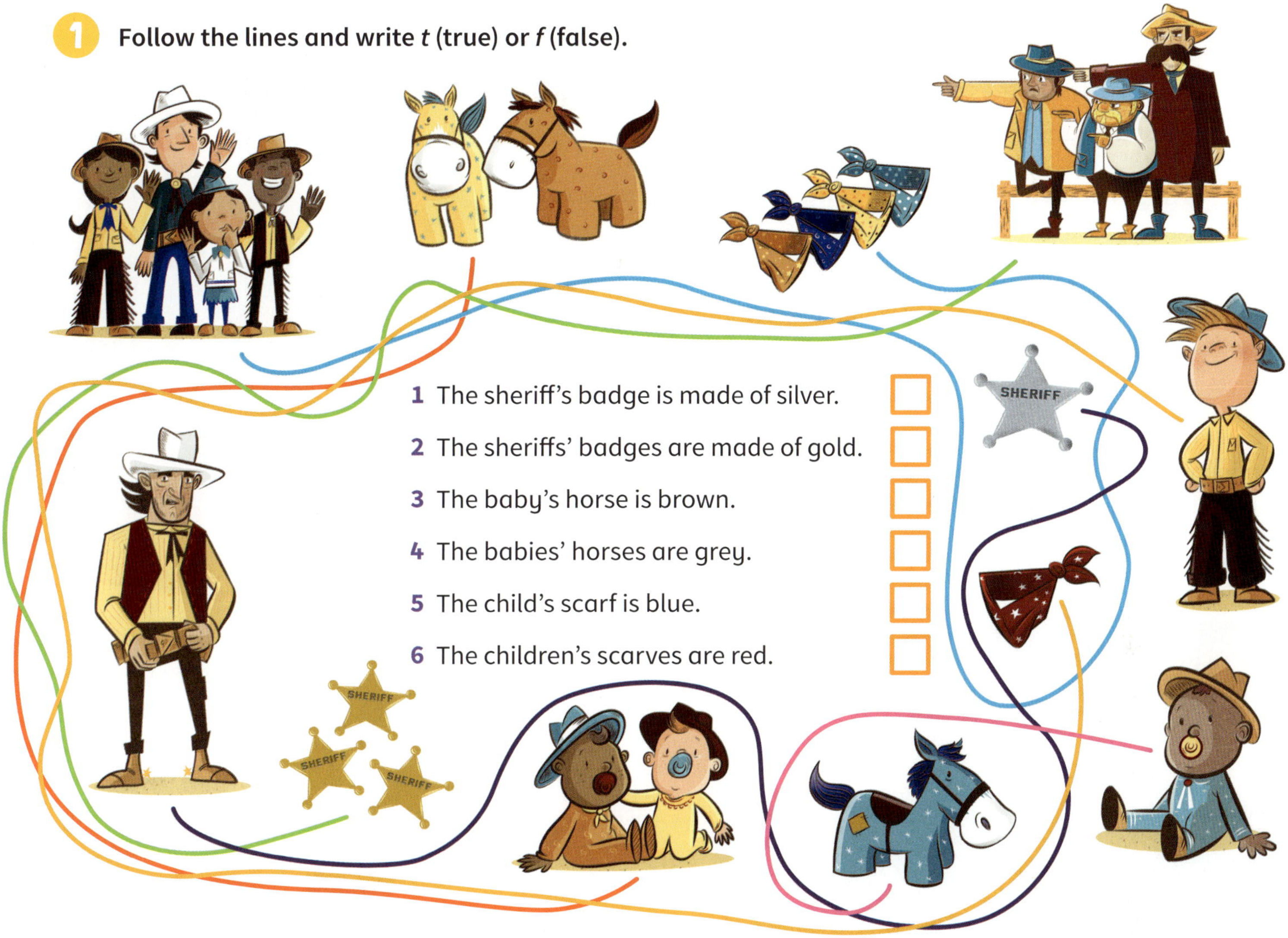

1 The sheriff's badge is made of silver. ☐
2 The sheriffs' badges are made of gold. ☐
3 The baby's horse is brown. ☐
4 The babies' horses are grey. ☐
5 The child's scarf is blue. ☐
6 The children's scarves are red. ☐

2 **Add ' to each sentence.**

1 This cowboys horse is brown.
2 These cowboys horses are brown.
3 This childs badge is made of gold.
4 These childrens badges are made of gold.

3 061 **Watch, listen and say.**

Language focus

I've got a **sheriff's** badge. They've got their **robbers'** badges.

Where's this **baby's** hat? They've got all the **babies'** hats.

4 **Look at the picture on page 58 and write sentences. How many sentences can you write in three minutes?**

- the robbers
- the sheriff
- the children

The robbers' horses are ...

The bank robbery

1 **Go through the story quickly and find answers to the questions.**

1 What are the names of the robbers?

2 What does the sheriff give the kids?

2 062 **Read and listen to the story to check your answers.**

The children watched the men get off their horses and walk up to the bank. The people in the street looked very worried and went inside their houses. The men had scarves around their mouths. They disappeared inside the bank.

'I don't like this,' said Phoebe. 'I think they're going to rob the bank.' A minute later, a woman ran out of the building. 'They're robbing the bank!' she shouted. 'You were right, Phoebe,' said Alex, 'but what can we do?' 'We can go in and stop them,' said Patrick. 'Don't be silly,' said Phoebe. 'That's too dangerous. Let's go and talk to the sheriff.'

The kids went into the sheriff's office and told him about the robbers. He wasn't very interested. 'Aren't you going to do something?' asked Phoebe. 'What can I do?' asked the sheriff. 'They're the Dalton brothers, the most dangerous robbers around. I'm not going to try to stop them. It's too dangerous!' 'Well somebody has got to do something,' said Patrick. 'Come on, I've got a plan!'

Patrick walked over to the robbers' horses. Phoebe and Alex followed. 'Pass me that rope,' he said. Alex gave him the rope and Patrick tied it around the horses' legs. 'That'll stop them!' he said. 'I think we need to do more' said Alex. 'Give me your penknife, Patrick.' 'Hurry up boys,' said Phoebe. 'The Daltons are coming.'

The Dalton brothers walked up to the children. 'You three are brave,' the tallest one said. He took out a big knife. The kids were scared. 'Don't worry,' he said. 'This is to free our horses. Nice try, kids!' He cut the rope from the horses' legs and they rode away. 'That wasn't a very good plan!' Phoebe said. 'Just wait a minute,' said Alex.

As the Daltons were leaving town, their horses jumped over a fence and the men fell to the ground. 'We've got them!' Alex shouted. 'Get the sheriff.'

The sheriff walked up to the brothers and put handcuffs on them. 'That was very clever, kids, but how did you do it?' 'I knew they had to jump over that fence to leave town,' said Alex, 'so I cut the straps on their saddles.'

The sheriff took the brothers to the jail and put them behind bars. He gave each of the kids a badge. 'Thank you!' he said. As the kids walked past the jail door, the shortest of the brothers shouted out to them. 'We'll get you kids!'

'I don't think so!' said Phoebe. She could see the yellow light glowing. 'Goodbye, Dalton brothers. Goodbye, Sheriff!' The Time Travellers walked into the light and were gone in a flash.

3 Choose the correct answers.

1 Who wants to go into the bank?
   a Alex   b Patrick   c Phoebe
2 Why doesn't the sheriff want to do anything?
   a He's scared.   b He's lazy.   c He's tired.
3 What does the tallest Dalton brother think of the kids?
   a They are silly.
   b They are courageous.
   c They are scared.
4 What does Alex do with the penknife?
   a He cuts the rope.
   b He stops the sheriff.
   c He cuts the saddles.

4 Who do you think says these things? Where and when do they say them?

1 Everybody on the floor! Now give us the money!
2 The Dalton brothers aren't scared of me!
3 That was a great plan, Alex.
4 Those kids. They tricked us!
5 These brothers aren't going to rob any more banks now.

1 Read the magazine article and match the words with the sentences.

1 teepee	a areas of land where modern Native Americans live
2 Sioux	b an animal that lives in North America
3 bison	c a famous Native American tribe
4 reservations	d a typical Native American house

Sitting Bull was a famous chief of the Sioux tribe.

The NATIVE AMERICANS

The first Europeans arrived in North America in 1492 and soon met the Native American people living there. The Europeans thought they were in India so they called these people Indians.

There were millions of Native Americans and they lived in many different tribes. Each tribe was different. They had different languages and lived in different types of houses. They loved their land and nature was important to them.

The Native Americans were friendly to the Europeans and helped them with their new lives. Soon more and more Europeans arrived in North America. Some Europeans didn't like the Native Americans because they were very different. Some wanted the Native Americans' land so they could build their homes and towns. There was fighting and many people were killed.

There are still many Native Americans living in North America. Although some live in cities and towns, many live in areas of land called reservations. They have their own schools and their own police.

Native Americans got food and clothes from bison.

Many Native Americans lived in tall tents called teepees.

2 Read the article again and answer the questions.

1 Why were Native Americans called Indians?
2 How were Native American tribes different?
3 What problems did the Europeans and the Native Americans have?
4 What is life like now for Native Americans?

1 063 **Listen and complete the place names.**

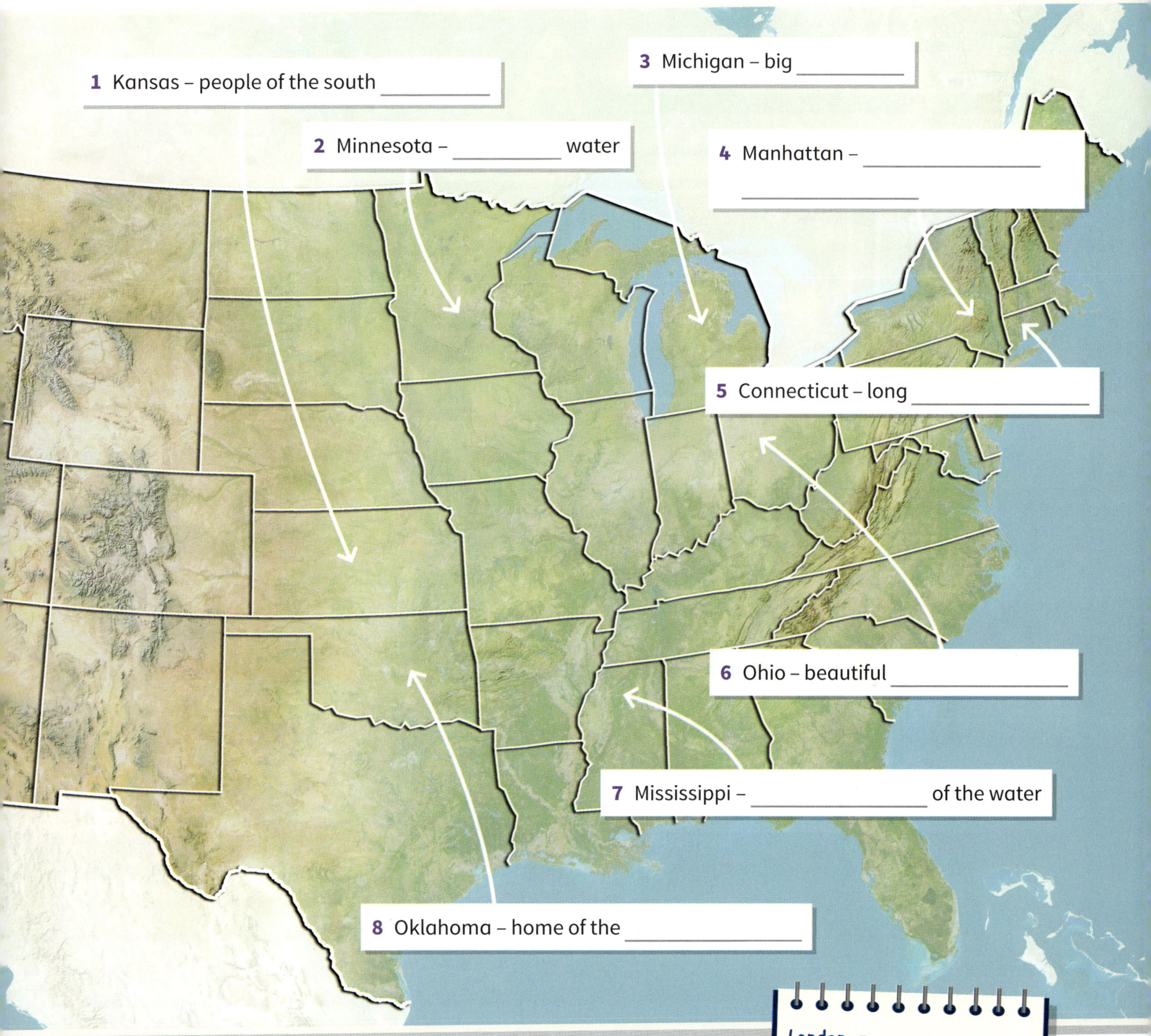

2 **Think of five places you know. Think of how to describe them.**

3 **Read your place names for your partner to guess.**

City with beautiful opera house.

Is it Sydney?

London –
place of many people

Paris –
city with big tower

Rio de Janeiro –
place of beautiful beaches

Materials used by Native Americans

What materials did Native Americans use?

1 064 Listen and number the photos.

stone

leather

animal bone

wood

2 What do you think these Native American objects are made of? Look and write the names of the materials.

1 
______

2 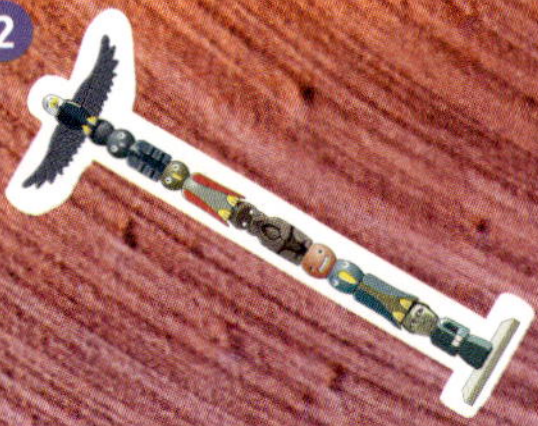
______

3 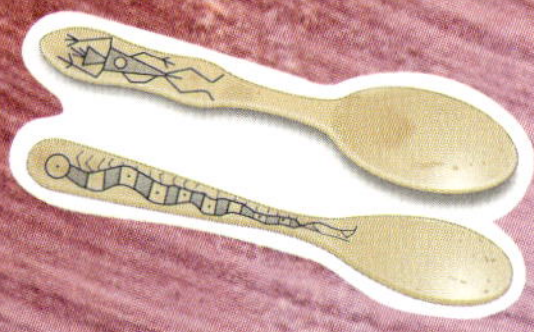
______

4 
______

3 Read and talk about the different Native American objects.

Tepees are made of leather because it's soft and strong, and waterproof.

NATIVE AMERICAN OBJECTS	MADE OF...	SOFT	HARD	STRONG	WATERPROOF
belts, bags, clothes, tepees	leather	✓		✓	✓
boxes, boats, barrels, totem poles	wood	✓	✓	✓	✓
spoons, forks, bracelets, toys	animal bones		✓		✓
arrows, knives, plates, bowls	stone		✓	✓	✓

4 Look at some other objects made by Native Americans and match.

1 This rug is made of strong grasses.
2 This flute is made of bones.
3 The drum is made of leather and wood.
4 This colourful bracelet is made of glass beads.
5 These snow shoes are made of wood and leather.

Super fact!

Bison were important to Native Americans. They used bison leather and bones to make many objects and they ate bison meat. There aren't many bison left in America now, so Native Americans use different materials to make things.

a

b
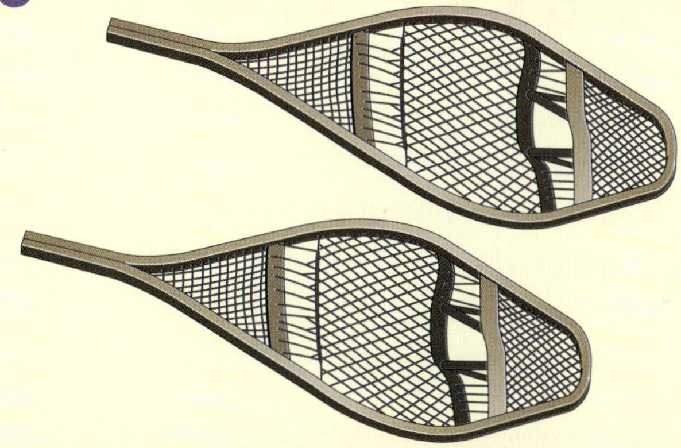

c

d
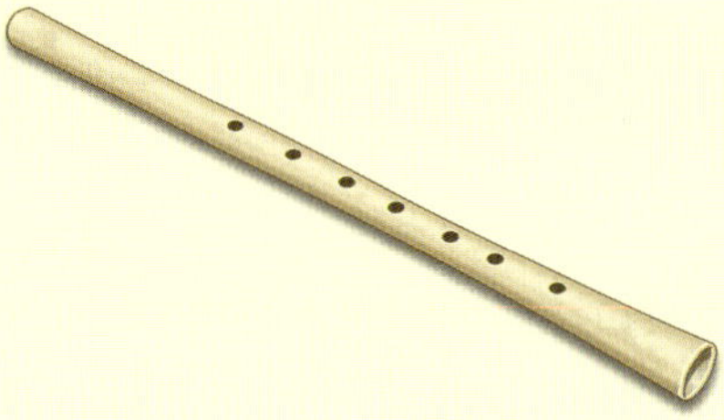

e
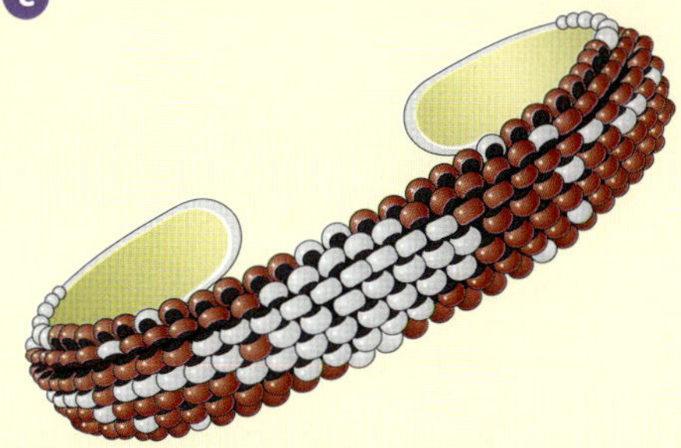

The rug is soft and strong. It isn't waterproof.

5 Look and say. Are they hard/soft/strong/waterproof?

6 Project Make a leaflet about a material that Native Americans used.

- Find a photo or draw and label the material.
- Draw and label some things that they made with it.
- Write a sentence about why they used this material? Is it soft/hard/strong/waterproof?

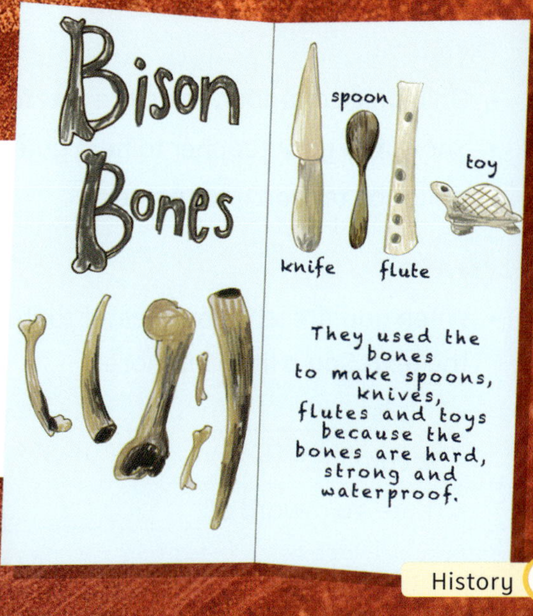

Time to present

A wanted poster

1 065 **Look at the poster and listen to the presentation. Make a note of three differences you hear.**

BETTY THE COYOTE

21 years old. 1.78 metres tall. Dark brown hair. Round face. Green eyes. Small nose. Bad teeth. Sometimes wears a red scarf and a black belt made of leather. Carries two pistols in brown holsters. Bring Betty the Coyote to any sheriff in Arizona. 500 dollars are waiting for you.

2 **Prepare and give a presentation.**

Think about it

- Work with a friend. Think of a name for the person on your Wanted poster.
- Draw a picture of the person. Think about what the person looks like and what clothes he or she wears.
- Draw a picture of the person on a big piece of paper. Colour it in.
- Make notes about the person, where he or she is from, his or her clothes, other things he or she has got (horse? pistols?).
- Think of how much the sheriff will pay for the person on your Wanted poster.

Prepare it

- On a piece of paper, write the text for your poster with your partner.
- Show it to your teacher to help you with the language.
- Write the text on your poster.

Present it

- When you present your poster to the class, do not just read out the text. Say a little bit more.
  - This is ___________.
  - Be careful!
  - There's a reward of ___________.

Presenting tip

When you give a presentation, you should speak a little bit louder than normal. Make sure everybody in your class can hear and understand what you are saying.

Think and write

Write a story

1 **Complete the story with the correct sentences.**

a 'Everybody give me your money!' he shouted loudly.

b 'Who did this?' he shouted angrily.

c 'I'll get Hank Knife, and I'll put him behind bars!' he said.

d 'He's so mean, and he's very dangerous!' they said.

Hank Knife was a robber who lived in Sandhill. Everyone was afraid of him. **(1)** ________
It was a Friday. There were lots of people in the street. Suddenly they saw Hank Knife on his big, black horse. He stopped in front of the bank and went inside. **(2)** ________ The people gave him all their money.
But Sandhill had a new sheriff. He wasn't afraid of Hank Knife. **(3)** ________
When Hank Knife came back to his horse, there was a rope around the horse's legs. Hank was angry. **(4)** ________ Then he bent down to cut the rope. The sheriff jumped out from behind a barrel. He arrested Hank Knife.

2 **Choose the best title for the story.**

Sandhill on a Friday

THE BIG BLACK HORSE

A lot of money

Bad luck for HANK KNIFE

3 **Look at the questions and write a story with the title 'Boris's last robbery'.**

- Who is the main character of the story?
- What does he do?
- What happens?

4 **In pairs, read your stories. How are they different?**

Writing tip

Make your story interesting. Write three or four sentences to say what people said, shouted or asked. Remember to use speech marks.

6 In Istanbul

1 066 **Listen and say the words. Check with your partner.**

1 flag
2 plate
3 carpet
4 sunglasses
5 cup and saucer
6 cushion
7 rings
8 comb
9 soap
10 basket
11 earrings

Istanbul is one of the world's biggest and most beautiful cities. It is the only city in the world that is built on two continents – Europe and Asia. They are divided by a bit of the sea that looks like a river: the Bosphorus Strait. Tourists love Istanbul because it offers the combination of a modern, Western lifestyle with fascinating Eastern traditions. In 2010, Istanbul was named the European Capital of Culture.

BIG QUESTION What can we buy in different countries?

2 067 **Read, listen and answer the questions.**

1 What does Patrick want to buy and why?
2 Why does Alex think that's not a good idea?
3 Which two continents are the children in?
4 How does Phoebe know where they are?

3 **Choose a word. Draw it for your partner to guess. Can you think of any other things you can buy?**

Is that a … ?

1 Read the website for tourists. Then cover it up and complete the sentences.

1 You should ________________ comfortable shoes.

2 You should always ________________ the name and address of your hotel on a piece of paper.

3 You shouldn't worry if you don't ________________ Turkish. Many people speak English.

4 You should ________________ a map when you walk around the city.

5 You shouldn't ________________ photos without asking.

What you should know about a holiday in ISTANBUL

- You should wear comfortable shoes all the time. You'll do lots of walking. It's easier in the right shoes!
- Make sure you know the name and the address of your hotel – write it on a piece of paper – Istanbul is a huge city. It's easy to get lost.
- You shouldn't worry if you don't speak Turkish. Many Turkish people speak very good English and are very friendly and helpful. But why don't you learn a few words in Turkish? People will like that!
- You should always take a map with you before you start walking around the city. And before you leave your hotel, you should make a plan of what you want to see.
- You shouldn't take photos without asking.

2 068 Watch, listen and say.

Language focus

When you come to my jungle, there are things you **should** try.

When you come to my jungle, there are things you **shouldn't** do.

3 Make some fun rules for your classroom.

You shouldn't talk to the students here. They bite!

You should bring an umbrella. It often rains here.

My world: buying presents

1 **Look at the objects in the shop window. Who would you buy these presents for and why?**

2 069 **Read and listen to the dialogue. Which present do they choose?**

Dad Let's get Mrs Thomas a present.
Ruby Mrs Thomas – our neighbour! Why?
Dad Because she's looking after your rabbit while we're on holiday.
Ruby Yes, that's a good idea. But what should we get her?
Dad What about a nice cushion like this one?
Ruby I'm not so sure. It's a bit silly. We should get her a key ring. This is nice.
Dad Perhaps we shouldn't. It's a bit tacky.
Ruby OK, what else is there?
Dad How about this cup? It's really nice and not too expensive.
Ruby OK. I think she'll like that.
Dad Perfect!

3 **Practise the dialogue in pairs.**

4 **Work in pairs to make your own dialogue.**

1 Choose one of these people with a friend:

a teacher *a friend* *a neighbour*

2 Decide why you want to buy this person a present.
3 Make a short dialogue about choosing a present.
4 Act out your dialogue to the class.

What to say

Making suggestions
Let's …
What about … ?
We should …
How about … ?

1 070 Read and listen to the dialogues. Match them with the pictures.

☐ **A** Could I see that ring over there, please?
B Of course.

☐ **A** Do you mind if I open this book?
B Not at all.

☐ **A** Do you mind if I try this jacket on?
B Not at all.

☐ **A** Could I buy some stamps for these postcards, please?
B Of course.

2 Complete the sentences with words from Activity 1.

1 ________ ________ see that cushion over there, ________?

2 ________ you ________ ________ ________ try these sunglasses on?

3 071 Watch, listen and say.

Language focus

Do you mind if I ask you a question?	Not at all.
Could you show me the way to the lake, please?	Yes, of course.
Could you help me carry my bag?	Yes, all right.
Could I take a selfie, please?	OK. Say 'Cheese!'

4 Choose a picture from Activity 1 and write a mini dialogue.

- Could you show me / tell me / give me … ?
- Could I see / have … ?
- Do you mind if I try this on / look at the … ?

LOST IN THE CITY

1. Look at the pictures. What do you think happens to Phoebe in the story?

2. 072 Read and listen to the story to check your answers.

Phoebe bought a little guidebook about Istanbul from the tourist office. The Time Travellers sat down to read it. 'Let's go sightseeing!' said Phoebe. She was so excited. The photos in her book were wonderful. 'This city's great!' Patrick said. 'Let's go!' They made a list of all the sights they wanted to see. 'We should go by underground,' said Phoebe. 'This city's so big, we can't walk all day.'

The nearest underground station was called Taksim. It was full of people and hard to move quickly. 'There's the train! Quick!' Patrick shouted. Patrick and Alex pushed through the crowd and jumped onto the train. Phoebe wasn't fast enough. The doors closed before she could get in! She didn't know what to do. 'Stop!' she shouted, but that didn't help.

Alex and Patrick talked about what to do. How would they find Phoebe in a city of more than 12 million people? 'Let's go and see all the sights we wanted to see,' Patrick said. 'Phoebe knows what they are. I'm sure we'll find her at one of them!' The boys spent six hours in Istanbul. They visited the Blue Mosque with its beautiful blue tiles. They visited the Bosphorus Bridge and the Spice Market, but they didn't find Phoebe. They were really worried.

'Can I help you?' a voice said. 'I'm Ali.' Ali was about the same age as them, and he was very friendly. Alex and Patrick told him what had happened. 'Hm! You lost your friend at the underground station in Taksim. She's probably waiting for you there!' he said. 'Of course!' Alex and Patrick shouted. 'Let's go back to Taksim!'

Sure enough, when the three boys arrived at Taksim they found Phoebe waiting on the platform where they had last seen her.

'I'm so sorry!' Patrick said. 'It wasn't very clever that we got on the train without you!' Phoebe laughed. 'I'm so happy we're together again. So happy! But what did you do all day?' The boys told her about all the beautiful places. 'I'd love to see them too!' Phoebe said. 'We can go and see them tomorrow!' said Ali. 'That's a great idea,' said Phoebe, 'but we can't stay!' 'Why not?' asked Ali. 'Istanbul is beautiful!' 'I know,' Phoebe said sadly. She was looking up towards the escalator where there was a yellow glow.

Ali was unhappy to say goodbye. He saw his three new friends going up the escalator. They waved at him. Then they slowly moved into the light and were gone in a flash.

3 Correct the mistakes in the sentences.

1 Phoebe, Alex and Patrick looked at a book with some photos of the underground.
2 They decided to travel around the city by bus.
3 Alex and Patrick went to see some sights. They wanted to find Ali, their friend.
4 They went back to Taksim with a Turkish girl.
5 When they arrived at Taksim, they couldn't find Phoebe.
6 Ali wanted to show Phoebe the city the next day, but she didn't like Istanbul.

4 Look at the picture and answer the questions with the phrases in the box.

in front of | behind | to the left of | to the right of

Where is the

- hotel?
- factory?
- souvenir shop?
- fire station?

Alex and Patrick now turn to face the left. Now where are the buildings?

1 073 **Match the flags with the countries. Listen and check.**

1 India
2 Indonesia
3 China
4 Japan
5 the USA
6 Germany

2 **Read the blog. Find one thing that comes from each country in Activity 1.**

Do you dream of travelling around the world and visiting countries that are far away? Well, maybe they're closer than you think. Have a look around your room. Look at the cool trainers on your floor (the ones your mum's always asking you to tidy away). They're made in Indonesia, which is on the other side of the world. Your jeans and T-shirt? They come from India. Now find your mobile phone. Look under the bed. There it is. That's made from hundreds of different parts from all over the world. Your computer? That came all the way from China.

Now your mum's home from work in her new car. That was made in Germany and then put on a ship and brought here. Your homework is done. You're tired and you need to relax. You lie back on your bed and turn on the TV (which came from Japan). There's a French film on, but you're too tired to read the subtitles. So you change the channel and watch an American police series. Who needs to travel the world? It's all here in your home.

3 **Read the text again and decide on the best title.**

1 The world in your room
2 Why is your room always such a mess?
3 Made in China.

4 **Work in pairs. Investigate where your things were made.**

1 Think about the things around you. Predict which country the most things were made in.
2 Look at five objects around you. Find out where they were made.
3 Write where the objects came from on the board to make a class list.
4 Which country were the most things made in? Was your prediction correct?

1 074 **Listen and draw lines from the countries to the food.**

1

2

3

4

Total food miles ________

a
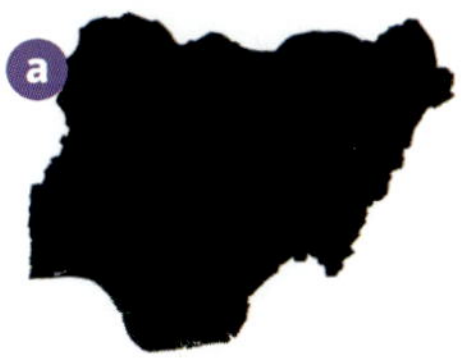
Nigeria [ ]

b

Spain [ ]

c

The USA [ ]

d

South Africa [ ]

e

Argentina [ ]

2 075 **How many miles has the food come? Listen again and write the numbers in the boxes. What is the total?**

3 **Discuss in small groups.**

1 What food that you eat comes from other countries?
2 What food that you eat definitely comes from your country?
3 What advantages are there to eating food that travels a long way?
4 What disadvantages are there to eating food that travels a long way?

Oranges come from …

… is a food that comes from our country.

4 **Find out where all the food for your breakfast comes from and how far it has to travel. Write a short paragraph.**

For breakfast today, I had a bowl of cereal with milk and a banana. The cereal came from the USA. The banana came from Brazil, but the milk came from my own country.

Marbling

What are some traditional arts?

Super fact!

It takes two years to learn how to be an Ebru artist.

1 076 Listen and number the photos.

marbling

Turkish marbled paper

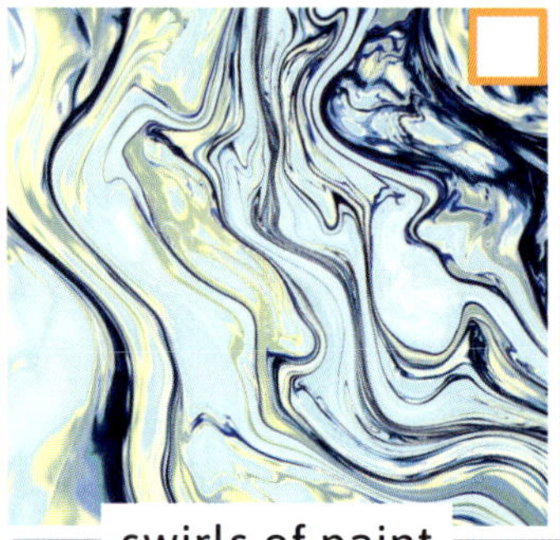
swirls of paint

artist's oil

2 Read about the art of paper marbling. Match the pictures with the instructions.

Paper marbling is a kind of art that is sometimes made in Turkey. Turkish artists use paper, oil, water and paint to make art in bright colours. In Turkey, this is called Ebru marbling. Ebru means 'cloud art'. Turkish artists can make amazing patterns, flowers and leaves by marbling.

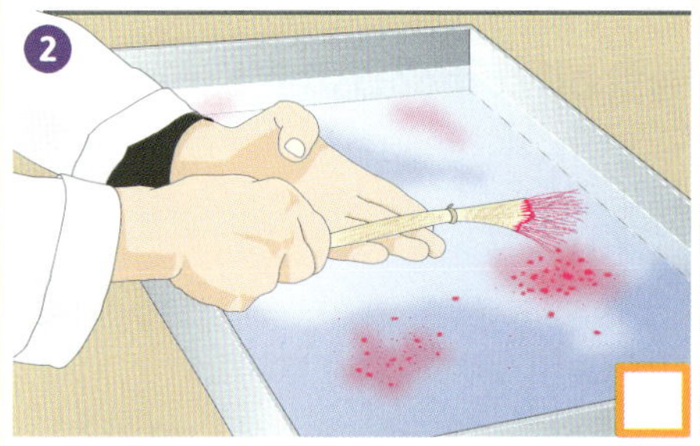

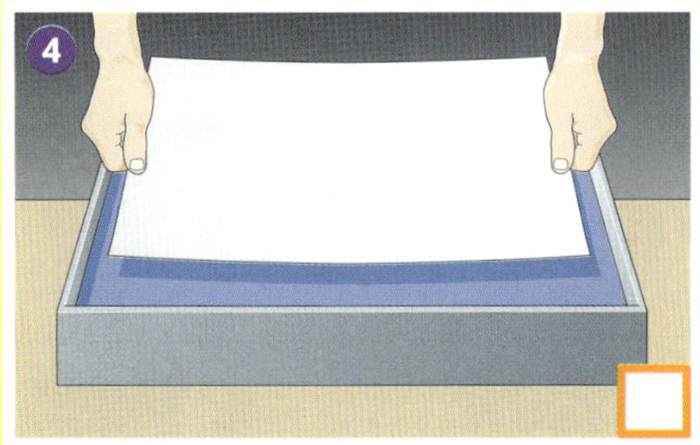

- **a** After that, the artist puts paper into the water.
- **b** First, the artist puts some artist's oil in a bowl of water.
- **c** The artist takes the paper out of the water.
- **d** Next, the artist uses a comb to make swirls of paint.
- **e** The oil and paint made a beautiful marbled pattern.
- **f** Then, the artist uses a brush to drop some paint on the water.

3 077 **Read about *suminagashi* and write the words. Listen and check your answers.**

blow paint leaf pattern

In Japan, marbling is called *suminagashi*, which means 'floating ink'. Japanese artists drop ink into the water, not **(1)** __________. The artists watch the **(2)** __________ that the ink makes and drop more ink into the water. Sometimes the Japanese artists **(3)** __________ the ink to make it move. Sometimes they use some hair or a **(4)** __________ to make beautiful patterns in the ink.

4 **Show how paper marbling is the same and different in Turkey and Japan. Write the numbers in the Venn diagram.**

1 Artists use paper and water.
2 Artists use a hair or leaf to make patterns.
3 Artists often use bright colours.
4 Artists put paper on top of the water.
5 Artists use a comb to make swirls.
6 The name means 'cloud art'.
7 The name means 'floating ink'.

Paper Marbling

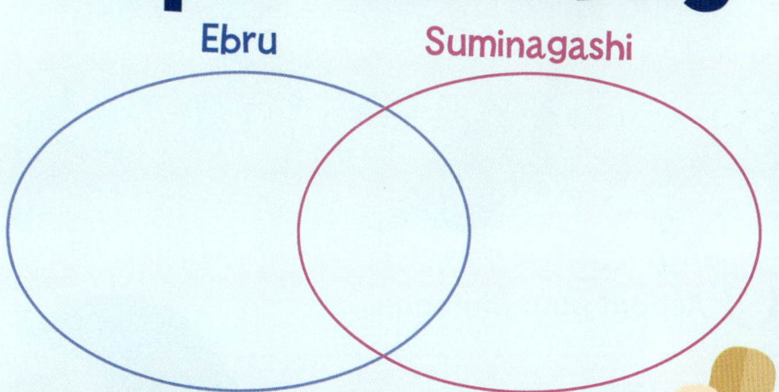

5 **Project** **Make some marbled paper.**

You need:

- A large bowl with about 10 cm of water in it
- Some oil
- Two or three different colour paints
- Two or three paint brushes
- A piece of white paper
- A clean stick or pencil

What to do:

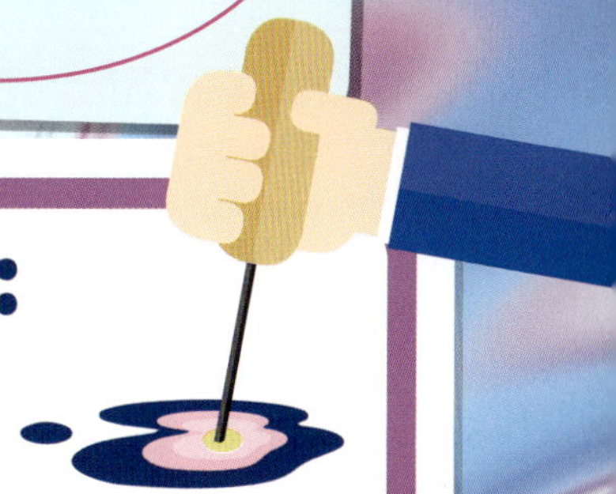

1 Drop a little oil into the water.
2 Put some paint on the first paintbrush.
3 Slowly drop a little paint into the water and watch it move.
4 Put a different colour paint on the second paintbrush.
5 Slowly drop a little of this paint into the water.
6 Take the stick or pen and use it to make patterns in the water.
7 Put a piece of paper on top of the water and then take the paper out of the water.
8 Look at your art. You can use it to cover your book.

Get talking

At a clothes shop

1 Choose a role card. Read and plan.

Student A

You are the customer.

You want to buy some clothes.
Think about the following:

- what you would like to buy
- how much the item costs
- whether they have got the item in another colour or another size
- if you can try it on
- what the item is made of

Student B

You are a shop assistant.

You ask/tell the customer

- what they would like to buy
- how much the item is
- if you have the item in another size and colour
- where they can try the item on
- what the item is made of

2 Act out your dialogue.

Student A

I'm looking for …
How much is/are … ?
Could you show me a different … ?
Have you got it in another … ?
Do you mind if I … ? / Can I … ?
What is it … ?

Student B

I can show you …
It's/They're …
Here we've got …
No problem.
I'll check if …
Come this way.
It's made of …

Think and write

A leaflet giving advice

1 Gavin is a new member of the basketball team. The trainer has written some tips for him. Write *should or shouldn't*.

TIPS FOR BECOMING A BASKETBALL STAR!

- Practice is on Monday and Friday. All team members **(1)** __________ be at the sports hall by 5 p.m. Training starts at 5.15 p.m.
- You **(2)** __________ always be friendly with the other team members. We can only become a good team if we are friends.
- You **(3)** __________ worry if you make mistakes.
- You **(4)** __________ be unfair. Basketball is a sport!

2 Make notes to complete the table.

Tips for visiting our town

Places to visit or not to visit:	Money and what to buy:
1 ____________	1 ____________
2 ____________	2 ____________
3 ____________	3 ____________
The weather and clothes to wear:	**Where and how long you stay:**
1 ____________	1 ____________
2 ____________	2 ____________
3 ____________	3 ____________

3 Write a leaflet giving advice to a visitor to your town.

What to say

Before you start writing, take time to think. Make notes.
Think about:

- places they should visit.
- places they shouldn't visit.
- the weather and what clothes they should wear.
- how much money they should bring and what they should buy.
- where they should stay.
- how long they should stay.

7 The story teller

1 078 **Listen and say the words. Check with your partner.**

1 lute
2 candles
3 mask
4 wig
5 actor
6 tights
7 costume
8 audience

William Shakespeare (1564–1616) is one of the world's most famous writers. He lived in England all his life and wrote lots of plays and poems. You can see his plays today in theatres all over the world. One of his most famous plays is *Romeo and Juliet.* It's a sad story about a boy and a girl who are in love, but their families are enemies.

BIG QUESTION What do we know about the theatre?

2 079 **Read, listen and complete the sentences.**

1 Alex thinks the theatre is ________________.
2 Mrs Butler showed them photos of ________________ and the Globe ________________.
3 The audience ________________ the play.
4 Phoebe thinks the play is ________________.

3 **Choose a word. Describe it for your partner to guess.**

> These people are in films and plays.

1 080 Read and listen to the dialogue. Who brings each item? Write the names below the items.

Paul What do we need for the play?

Lisa We need costumes, two wigs, a necklace and a bracelet for the queen and a sword for the king. I'll bring the costumes.

Daisy I'll bring a blonde wig from my grandmother.

Harry I think we've got a black wig at home. I'll ask my mum if I can have it.

Lisa Great. What about the necklace and the bracelet?

Adam I'll check at home. I'm sure my sister has got lots of them.

Lisa Excellent. What about a sword?

Lily I'll make one.

Paul I'll bring some hats. We've got lots of old ones at home.

Lisa Great. Thank you all. See you tomorrow at three.

1

2
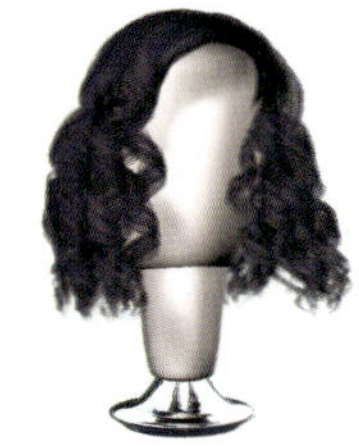

3

4

5

6

2 Complete and say the sentences with *'ll* and the verb in brackets.

1 I a wig. (bring)

2 I a sword. (make)

3 I at school. (check)

4 I my sister. (ask)

3 081 Watch, listen and say.

Language focus

Why don't we do a jungle show for everyone to see?
Great idea! I**'ll build** a stage right there by the tree.
And then I**'ll get** the monkeys to sing a funny song.
We**'ll ask** the snake to join in too and bring his friends along.

4 Work with your partner. How can you help them? Then swap roles.

- I'm thirsty.
- I can't do my homework
- This bag is very heavy.
- I'm hungry.
- It's cold in here.
- I can't find my camera.

I'm thirsty.

I'll get you a glass of orange juice.

1 082 **Listen and correct the mistakes. Then sing the song.**

I'll buy you a ~~parrot~~, **(1)** ____________
I'll buy you a nice hat,
I'll buy you a bracelet,
I'll buy you a car. **(2)** ____________

I really don't believe you,
When you promise me these things,
You'll never buy me necklaces,
You'll never buy me rings.

I'll write you a comic, **(3)** ____________
I'll tell you a secret,
I'll sing you a song,
I'll build you a house. **(4)** ____________

I really don't believe you,
When you promise me these things,
You'll never write me poems,
You'll never buy me rings.

I'll take you to the circus, **(5)** ____________
I'll take you to the sea, **(6)** ____________
I'll take you to a show,
I'll do it all for you.

I really don't believe you,
When you promise me these things,
You'll never take me to a show,
You'll never buy me rings.

All about music: Duets

When two people sing a song together it is called a duet. Often the singers are a man and a woman and the songs are romantic ballads. These songs can be about happy times, but they are usually about when things go wrong.

What I think about this song

It's great. It's OK. I don't really like it.

Phonics

2 084 **Listen and say the dialogue.**

Olive Let's go to the Shakespeare Theatre!

George Isn't it a little expensive, dear?

Olive Yes, but I promise – you'll love it, George!

George Err … of course I will, Olive.

1 What are the actors doing? Match the pictures with the sentences.

1 He's just read some good news.
2 He's just heard some bad news.
3 He's just cut his finger.
4 She's just dropped a book on her foot.
5 She's just got up.
6 She's just had a fright.

2 085 Watch, listen and say.

Language focus

I**'ve just heard** the explorer. Listen!
He**'s just fallen** over a tree. Look!
They**'ve just dropped** some nuts on him.
He**'s just shouted** at them. See?

3 Play the game. Mime and say.

HELPING SHAKESPEARE

1 **Go through the story quickly and find answers to the questions.**

1 How do the children think Shakespeare should change the end of his play?

2 What do the audience think of the new ending to the play?

2 **086** **Read and listen to the story to check your answers.**

'Let's go and talk to Shakespeare,' said Phoebe. 'I feel sorry for him.' 'How can we help him?' answered Alex. 'I've got an idea,' Phoebe said. The friends climbed up onto the stage. Shakespeare was sitting on a big box. The children said hello. 'I don't know what to do,' Shakespeare said. 'The audience didn't like my play. They shouted and threw eggs and vegetables onto the stage.' 'Maybe we can help you,' said Phoebe. 'I don't see how you can do that,' Shakespeare answered sadly.

Suddenly they heard shouting. 'Where is he? We want our money back!' Two men with big sticks were in the theatre looking for Shakespeare. They looked very angry. 'Stand at the edge of the stage,' said Patrick. 'Quickly, they're coming! When they're close, wave your arms in the air.' Shakespeare stood next to the box at the edge of the stage. Patrick picked up an actor's sword and he hid behind the box with Alex. When the two men saw Shakespeare, they ran up to him shouting, 'Give us our money back!'

The men ran towards Shakespeare. When they were very close, he waved his hands and Patrick tripped them with the sword. With a loud crash they fell off the stage. 'Run, or I'll get you with my sword,' Patrick shouted. The men ran away. They were very frightened. Shakespeare was happy. 'Thank you, you've just saved my life!' he said. 'Please come to my house and have dinner with me.'

At Shakespeare's house, the children and Shakespeare talked about *Romeo and Juliet*. 'Maybe the audience didn't like the happy ending,' Phoebe said. 'Why don't you rewrite the ending so that they both die? Maybe the audience will like that ending better.' At that moment, they heard voices outside.

Shakespeare opened the door. It was the men from the theatre with some of their friends. They looked very angry. 'That's him,' said one of the men pointing at Patrick. 'He's the one who had the sword.' They all started walking towards Patrick. 'Stop!' shouted Shakespeare. 'Leave the boy alone or you will never know the new ending of my play.' 'New ending?' said one of the men. 'What happens?' 'Come and see,' said Shakespeare 'There are free tickets for all of you.'

The Time Travellers watched from the side of the stage. The audience were enjoying the play and Shakespeare was very happy. At the end, the audience clapped. Shakespeare looked at the kids and waved his hand for them to join him on the stage. As they walked up to it, they saw the yellow glow in front of them. They stepped through and were gone in a flash.

3 Put the sentences in the correct order.

- ☐ Alex and Patrick save Shakespeare from the two men.
- ☐ Some angry men arrive at Shakespeare's house.
- ☐ Shakespeare invites the three friends for dinner.
- ☐ The three friends are in a theatre.
- ☐ The three friends talk to Shakespeare.
- ☐ Shakespeare offers some free tickets to the men.
- ☐ The audience do not like the ending of the play.
- ☐ Two men want their money back.
- ☐ The audience like the ending of the play.

4 Match the differences between Shakespeare's Globe and theatres now. Can you think of another difference?

Shakespeare's Globe

1. There were candles to light the stage.
2. The actors were all men.
3. Most of the audience stood up.
4. If the play was bad, people threw fruit.
5. Many theatres did not have a roof.

Theatres now

a. Everyone sits down.
b. Most theatres are inside.
c. There are electric lights.
d. Actors can be men or women.
e. If they do not like the play, people leave.

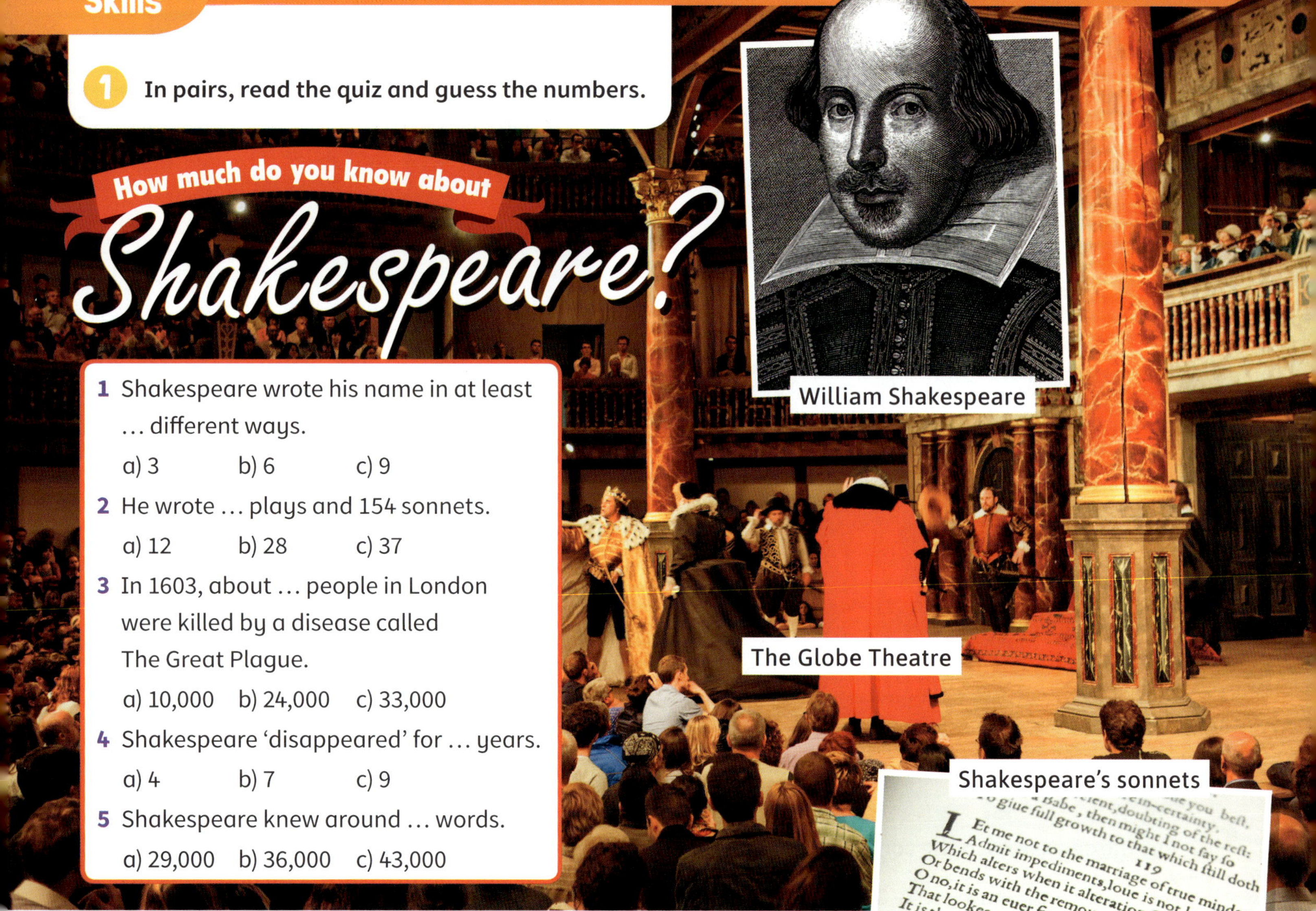

William Shakespeare

The Globe Theatre

Shakespeare's sonnets

1 In pairs, read the quiz and guess the numbers.

How much do you know about Shakespeare?

1 Shakespeare wrote his name in at least … different ways.
a) 3 b) 6 c) 9

2 He wrote … plays and 154 sonnets.
a) 12 b) 28 c) 37

3 In 1603, about … people in London were killed by a disease called The Great Plague.
a) 10,000 b) 24,000 c) 33,000

4 Shakespeare 'disappeared' for … years.
a) 4 b) 7 c) 9

5 Shakespeare knew around … words.
a) 29,000 b) 36,000 c) 43,000

2 087 Listen and check your answers.

3 Read about 50-word stories and think about the questions.

Can you write a story using exactly 50 words? Look at this example. It tells the story of Shakespeare's *Romeo and Juliet.* There is only one problem. It's got five words too many. Can you make it exactly 50 words long?

Romeo and Juliet fall in love. Their families are great enemies so they decide to get married in secret. Before this, Juliet pretends to die to avoid marrying a man she doesn't like very much. Romeo thinks she is dead and so he kills himself. Juliet wakes up, sees Romeo's dead body and kills herself.

4 Think of a story you know well and write it in 50 words.

5 Make notes and use them to tell your story to a group. Can they guess its title?

1 **Look at the pictures and answer the questions.**

1 What are the three men doing?
2 What does the man want to do with the cow?

2 088 **Read, listen and check your answers.**

Barney's fur

Marlowe was the richest man in the village. One evening, three men came to his house. They were tired and wanted a bed for the night.

'You can sleep in the stable,' said Marlowe, 'and my servant will bring you some soup.'

The three men said thank you and went to the stable, and the servant brought them the soup.

In the middle of the night, one of the men quietly got up. He took a rope and tied it round the cow's neck. He led the cow into a forest and tied it to a tree. 'I'll get the cow in the morning and sell her at tomorrow's market,' he thought.

Next morning, the servant went to the stable. When he saw that one cow was missing, he went to tell Marlowe. Marlowe went to the stable. 'Did you take one of my cows?' he asked.

'Of course not,' the three men answered. 'We were asleep all night.'

Marlowe told his wife about the cow. 'I'm sure that one of the three men took the cow.' She said, 'I have a plan.'

They went to the stable and she said, 'We have a very clever dog called Barney. Go into the room where Barney is and stroke him. When the thief touches Barney's fur, Barney will bark.'

The first man went into the room. The dog didn't make a sound. The second man went in. The dog didn't make a sound. Finally, the third man went in. The dog didn't make a sound.

'Did you all touch the dog's fur?' asked the woman. 'Yes,' they said. Then Marlowe's wife asked to smell the hand they used to touch the dog. She smelt them in turn. When she got to the third man, she smelt his hand and said, 'You are the thief. Your friends' hands smell of Barney. Your hand doesn't. You didn't touch Barney's fur. You didn't want Barney to bark. Now, please tell us where the cow is.'

3 **Match the sentence halves to make the summary.**

1 Three men were looking
2 Marlowe told them to sleep in the stable
3 In the middle of the night, one of the men
4 He wanted to sell it
5 In the morning, one of the servants
6 The farmer told his wife, who
7 The three men had to stroke
8 The thief's hand didn't
9 So the farmer's wife knew

a in the market the next day.
b smell of Barney.
c and gave them some soup.
d the dog's fur.
e who the thief was.
f had a plan.
g for a place to stay overnight.
h saw that a cow was missing.
i took Marlowe's cow into a forest.

Shakespeare's theatre

The Globe Theatre

What do we know about theatres?

1 089 Listen and number the photos.

make-up

special effects

history play

tragedy

characters props

comedy

Super fact!
Some make-up was made from mouse bones.

2 090 Read and listen to the interview about Shakespeare's theatre.

INTERVIEW

1 **TV Presenter** *What was it like inside The Globe Theatre?*

Actor It didn't smell good because the audience didn't wash often and they dropped food on the floor. The theatre was big and 3,000 people could watch a play there. The audience made a lot of noise.

2 **TV Presenter** *What kind of plays did people watch?*

Actor They watched history plays, comedies and tragedies.

3 **TV Presenter** *What costumes did the actors wear?*

Actor The actors were all men and they sometimes wore wigs and make-up. They put on very big wigs when they played important or famous characters.

4 **TV Presenter** *Did they have any special effects?*

Actor Yes. They had a thunder drum for thunder and they put special powder on candles to make them look like lightning.

What was the question? Write 1–4 beside the actor's words.

- ☐ They had a thunder drum.
- ☐ They wore big wigs to play important characters.
- ☐ It didn't smell good and it was very noisy.
- ☐ History plays, comedies and tragedies.

3 Talk to a partner. What do you think is interesting about theatres in Shakespeare's time?

I think it's interesting that the audience made a lot of noise.

Me too!

4 Match the props and what the actors used them for.

1 ☐ for acting a fight
2 ☐ for acting eating a meal
3 ☐ for playing a king or queen
4 ☐ for playing a rich woman
5 ☐ for playing someone badly hurt

5 Take turns to mime an action to a partner. Guess the action.

- **playing a musical instrument**
- **playing a board game**
- **fighting with a sword**
- **eating a meal**
- **riding a horse**
- **climbing a tree**

Are you playing a musical instrument?

Yes, that's right.

Sometimes actors didn't use props. They mimed the actions. When you mime, you use your hands and body to show the action.

6 Project Make a theatre stage in a box.

- Choose the kind of play that you want to show.
- Paint a scene at the back of the box.
- Draw and cut out some actors and their costumes.
- Make two or three props.
- Stick your actors and props on the stage.
- Tell your friends about the play, the characters and the props.

This is our stage. The play is a comedy. The characters are dancing after dinner. The actors are wearing make-up and wigs. The props are a table with some food on it.

Time to present

Class survey

1 091 **Listen to the presentation on books and look at the bar chart. Find two differences.**

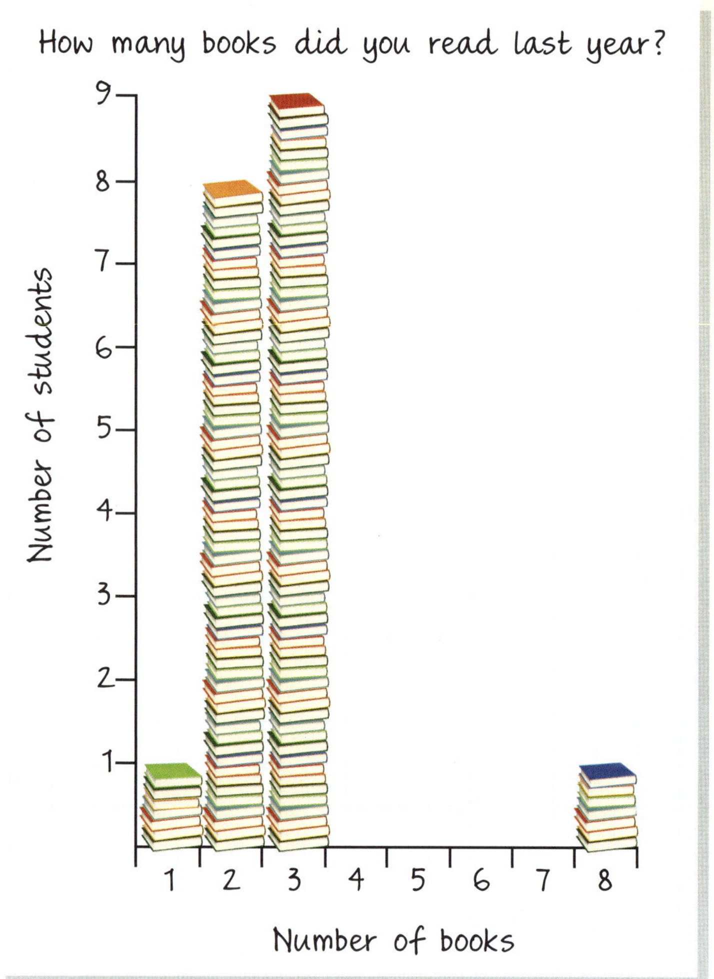

Presenting tip

Take your time to explain the bar chart. Make sure your classmates understand what each of the two lines mean. Write in big letters 'Number of students' / 'Number of books'.

2 092 **Match the sentence halves. Listen again and check.**

1 Here are
2 Let me explain
3 As you can see
4 A total of nine students
5 Thank you

a read three books.
b a few things.
c our results.
d for listening.
e from the bar chart.

3 **Complete a class survey.**

Think about it

- Who is your favourite writer?
- What is your favourite book?
- Is there a book you didn't like at all?
- What book are you reading at the moment?
- What was the last book you read?
- Where do you read? In your room? In the living room? Somewhere outside?
- How many hours do you read in a week?
- How many books did you read last year?

Prepare it

- Choose eight interviewers, one for each question.
- The interviewers walk around the class and ask everyone their question.
- The interviewers write down their classmates' answers.

Present it

- In groups, use the interviewers' notes to prepare a large bar chart for each question.
- Look at the example in Activity 1.
- Show the bar chart to the class and explain it.

Think and write

A biography

1 **Complete the biography of William Shakespeare with the phrases from the box.**

at the age of 18	he spent the rest of his life	He died in 1616
He was born in	In 1598	Between 1585 and 1592

Many people consider William Shakespeare to be the greatest writer in the English language. However, not a lot is known about his life. **(1)** ______________ 1564 in Stratford-upon-Avon in England. He was the third of seven children for his parents, John and Mary. He went to a good school and **(2)** ______________ he married Anne Hathaway. She was eight years older than him. They had three children.

(3) ______________, he started a successful theatre company in London where he wrote, produced and acted in his plays.

(4) ______________, his company moved to the famous Globe Theatre. In 1603, King James I gave his company royal support. In 1610, Shakespeare retired from the theatre and **(5)** ______________ in Stratford-upon-Avon. **(6)** ______________ at the age of 52.

2 **Answer the questions.**

1 How many brothers and sisters did Shakespeare have?
2 In what year did he get married?
3 How old was Anne when they married?
4 How old was Shakespeare when he returned to Stratford?

3 **Complete the sentences so that they are true about you.**

I was born ______________.
At the age of ________ I ______________.
In 20________ I ______________.
Between 20________ and 20________,
I ______________.

Writing tip

When you write a biography, make sure you put the facts in order. In a story, there is always a beginning, a middle and an end. In a story about a person's life, this is the same.

4 **Research a person you like and write a short biography for them. Use time phrases.**

8 Museum of the future

When we go to a museum, we see things from the past, and we learn about how people used to live. When you see a train or a plane in a museum, they look very different from the planes and trains of today. What will museums of the future show? They will show the planes and trains that we think are modern now. To visitors in the future these things will look old!

1 093 **Listen and say the words. Check with your partner.**

1 farmer
2 cleaner
3 engineer
4 dentist
5 artist
6 designer
7 computer programmer
8 mechanic
9 businesswoman
10 businessman

BIG QUESTION How will jobs change in the future?

2 094 **Read, listen and answer the questions.**

1 What did Phoebe's grandpa do?
2 Why is the museum strange?
3 What year is it?
4 How is the world different?

3 **Choose a word. Describe it for your partner to guess.**

He works with animals.

1 095 Listen to the advert. Colour the buttons.

2 096 Complete what the robot says. Then listen again and check.

1 If you're thirsty, I'll make you a nice cup of ______________________.
2 If your room is in a mess, I'll ______________________.
3 If you want to have fun, I'll ______________________.
4 If you're tired, I'll do ______________________.

3 097 Watch, listen and say.

Language focus

If I press the red button, it**'ll** clean the ground.

If I press the blue button, it**'ll** spin around.

If I press the green button, I don't know what it**'ll** do.

Oh no! Achoo!

4 Play the robot game with a partner.

1 **Look at the jobs. Answer the questions with a partner.**

1 Which jobs can be done by robots now?

2 Which jobs do you think will be done by robots in the future?

2 098 **Read and listen to the dialogue. Which jobs do they talk about?**

James What do you want to do when you're older?

Amelia I'm not really sure. Maybe I'll be a teacher.

James I don't think so. There won't be any teachers in the future.

Amelia Really? Why do you think that?

James There will just be robots. Robots will do everything. We won't need teachers.

Amelia I'm not sure. There are some things we need people for. Teaching is one of them.

James I hope you're right. I don't want you to study for a job that doesn't exist.

Amelia So what would you like to be when you're older?

James I'd like to be a robot designer. It's the only job we can be sure will exist.

Amelia Really? Maybe robots will start designing other robots.

James No way! If that happens, it'll be the end of the world.

3 **Practise the dialogue in pairs.**

4 **Work in pairs to make your own dialogue.**

1 With a friend, choose a job you want to do when you are older.

2 Decide what will happen to this job in the future.

3 Make a short dialogue about the job.

4 Act out your dialogue to the class.

What to say

Talking about the future

What do you want to do when you're older?

I want to be …

Maybe I'll be …

There won't be any …

I'd like to be a …

1 099 Read and listen to the dialogue. What will Pete do on Sunday?

Rich What can we do on Sunday?
Pete Let me think. Ah, I know. We can build a tree house.
Rich But what if it rains?
Pete Then we'll go to my room and listen to music.
Rich But what if I don't like your music?
Pete Then we'll play computer games.
Rich But what if your computer doesn't work?
Pete Then we'll have an ice cream!
Rich But what if it's too cold for an ice cream?
Pete Then we'll make some tomato soup.
Rich But what if you haven't got any tomatoes at home?
Pete Then we'll make some tea.
Rich But what if I don't want any tea?
Pete Oh, sorry, I've got no time on Sunday.
Rich Why's that?
Pete Because … if it's sunny, I'll build a tree house.
If it rains, I'll listen to …

2 100 Watch, listen and say.

Language focus

Let's cross the bridge.
But **what if** it breaks?
Then I'll catch you.
That's all it takes.

Let's cross the lake.
But **what if** we fall in?
That's not a problem.
Then we'll swim.

3 Read the examples and play the *But what if … ?* game.

Let's ride our bikes. Let's go to the zoo. Let's play football. Let's sing a song. Let's go for a walk. Let's help Dad.

Let's ride our bikes.
But what if it rains?
We'll get a bit wet.
But what if we get a cold?
We'll miss a few days of school.
But what if we miss an important exam?

THE TROUBLE WITH ORANGEHEAD XR-97

1 **Work in pairs. Look at the pictures and the title of the story.**

1 Write down words that come to your mind.

2 Make a story out of your words.

2 101 **Read and listen to the story to find out if it is similar to or different from your story.**

The children walked around the museum. There were some sports cars and motorbikes at the end of it. 'Amazing!' Alex thought. 'People don't use cars and motorbikes any more!' 'Boring,' said Patrick. 'I'm going.' 'Where?' shouted Phoebe. Patrick pointed at a door with a *Don't enter* sign on it. 'Let's open that door,' he said. 'Patrick, no!' said Phoebe.

Patrick didn't listen. He went into the room. Alex and Phoebe followed him. Inside, sat a big robot with an orange head. It was at a computer with its back to the children. 'Tomorrow, I'll be master of the world!' laughed the robot. The children were scared. 'What can we do?' Patrick whispered. 'Let's get out of here,' said Phoebe.

They left the room and heard a sound coming from a submarine. 'Help! Help me!' 'What's that?' Patrick asked. There was a man trapped inside. He looked very scared. 'How can we get him out?' asked Phoebe. Patrick ran towards the room with the models. A minute later, he was back with a big box of tools from the mechanic.

The children opened the door and set the man free. His name was Don and he was the programmer of the robots. 'Orangehead XR-97 was my best robot,' Don said sadly. 'But he's dangerous. He locked me in the submarine. He wants to take over the world. If we don't stop him, he will destroy everyone.' The children were very worried. 'What can we do?' asked Alex.

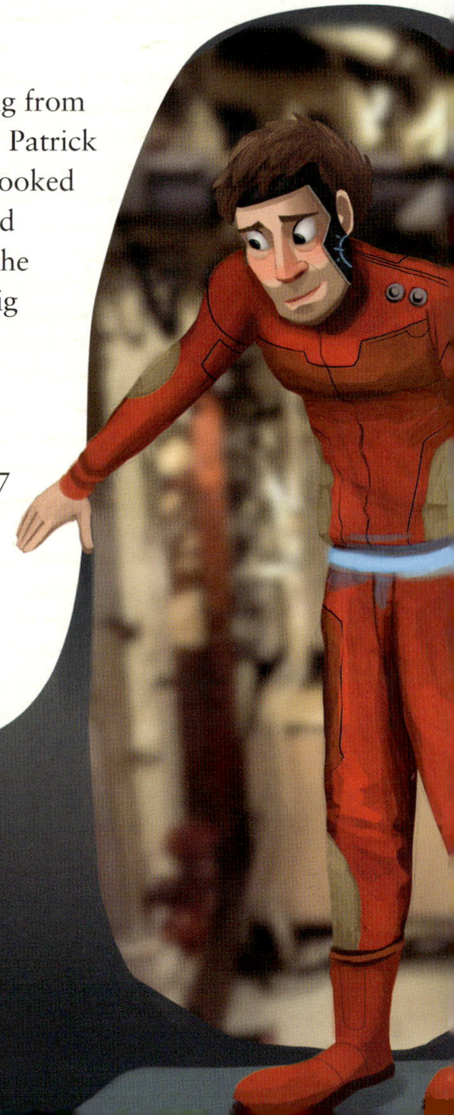

Don had an idea. 'Every morning from 6.55 to 7 o'clock, all the robots shut down for five minutes to charge their batteries. That's our only chance. But now we have to hide. Quick!'

'Hide? Where?' said Patrick. 'Get on a motorbike or in a car. But don't move,' said Don. Don climbed back into the submarine. When the robots came to clean the room, they saw two boys in the sports car and a girl on the motorbike, but they thought they were wax models.

The next morning at 6.55, Don and the children entered the computer room. It was full of very quiet robots, including Orangehead XR-97. Don switched on the computer and worked very quickly. At 7 o'clock, there was a loud noise. The Time Travellers saw flames and smoke coming out of Orangehead XR-97. 'I destroyed it!' Don said.

He turned around to thank the children and saw a bright glowing yellow light. The children waved goodbye and stepped into the light. They were gone in a flash.

3 **Complete the sentences. You can use 1, 2, 3 or 4 words.**

1 The kids saw a door with the *Don't enter* sign, but ________________.
2 They found out that the robot ________________ wanted to take over the world.
3 They went to a room and found a man ________________.
4 He told them that the robot with the orange head was his best robot, but ________________.
5 The robots ________________ to recharge their batteries.
6 Don didn't like it, but he had to ________________.

4 **Work in groups. Read and answer.**

1 Two fathers and two sons were making robots. Each of them made one robot. So why did they only have three robots when they finished?
2 A scientist made a robot that looked like a horse. He rode to town on Sunday, stayed two days, and left town on Sunday. How did he do it?

1 **Discuss in pairs.**

Look at the list of unusual jobs. One of them is not real. Which one do you think it is? What do you think the other jobs involve?

fruit cleaner

pet detective

elephant dancer

ostrich babysitter

pet-food tester

golf-ball diver

2 102 **Listen and check your answers.**

3 103 **Listen again. Decide if the sentences are *t* (true) or *f* (false). Correct the false ones.**

1 Pet-food testers don't usually eat the food. ☐
2 Fruit cleaners work in supermarkets. ☐
3 There is a film about a pet detective. ☐
4 Looking after ostriches is a very busy job. ☐
5 Golf-ball divers give the balls back to the golfers. ☐

4 **Work in pairs.**

1 Think of (or make up) a funny or unusual job. Think of what the job involves and give the job a name.
2 Tell the class about your job and decide on the best one.
3 Write a paragraph about your job.

Leaf cleaners clean leaves in gardens to make them look nice …

1 **Discuss in pairs.**

1 Think about fire fighters. What do they do?

2 Do you think they are usually men or women?

2 **Read the interview with a fire fighter. Does she like her job?**

1 ______________________________

My grandfather and my uncle were both fire fighters, so it's a job I know well. When I was little I always wanted to be a fire fighter. But when I grew up, I thought I was too short so I became a teacher.

2 ______________________________

One day, I took my class on a school trip to the fire station. I was really excited and I knew I wanted to do the job. A year later I was a fire fighter.

3 ______________________________

Well, he's a fire fighter too, so he understands the job. We work at different fire stations so we don't often see each other at work – only when there's a really big fire.

4 ______________________________

Lots of things. When I was a teacher, I always worked from 9a.m. until 3.30p.m. As a fire fighter, I work at very different times. It makes the job interesting. I also like the friends I have at the fire station.

5 ______________________________

No, I'm the only one. But I don't mind. I like being with the men. They're funny and we laugh a lot. But I think more women should become fire fighters. Women are as brave as men.

6 ______________________________

Knowing that you are doing an important job and saving lives. That makes you feel really good.

3 **Read again and write the questions in the correct places above.**

What does your husband think about the job?
So how did you get interested in fire fighting again?
And finally, what's the best thing about the job?
What do you like about the job?
Are there many women at your fire station?
Did you always want to be a fire fighter?

4 **Work in pairs.**

1 Write a list of three more jobs.

2 Are the jobs usually done by men or women?

3 What do you think about that? Do you think it will change in the future?

… are usually men/women.

I think that is because men/women …

I don't think that is right.

FARMING

traditional farming – how people farmed for hundreds of years, before machines

modern farming – new kinds of farming, using machines

How are jobs on farms changing?

Super fact!

Farming is very old. The first crops were farmed more than 11,000 years ago!

1 104 Listen and number the photos.

crops

polytunnel

chemicals

drone

machine

2 Look at the T-chart and complete with the lines below.

a don't use them to stop insects
b sometimes grow them inside a polytunnel
c collect them by hand
d water them with machines
e farmers watch the crops to see if they need water

	Traditional farming	Modern farming
1 vegetables	always grow vegetables in a field	
2 seeds	water seeds by hand	
3 crops		collect crops with machines
4 chemicals		use chemicals to stop insects eating the crops
5 drones		farmers use drones to watch crops and look after them better

3 Look at the T-chart again. Why do you think farmers prefer modern or traditional ways of farming? Use the words and phrases to help you.

quicker easier safer better for the environment cheaper more tiring

I think some farmers prefer to collect crops with machines because it's quicker.

4 Read and look. What are the farm workers doing?

Farm workers can use traditional or modern ways to look after crops and animals. Sometimes farm workers do different jobs, like making food and selling it in the farm shop.

In photo 1 she's …

5 105 Read about drones and fill in the gaps. Listen and check.

crops   photographs   help   machines   sky

Modern farm workers often use **(1)** ________________, like drones, to make their work easier. Drones take photographs from the **(2)** ________________. The **(3)** ________________ show farm workers when their crops need water. The photographs also show if the **(4)** ________________ have a disease, so they can use chemicals to help the plants. Farm workers can use the photographs to see if any animals need **(5)** ________________.

6 Project Design a new type of machine to help farmers in the future.

- Think of a problem farm workers can have.
- Design a machine to help them with this problem.
- Draw your machine.
- Write a description of your machine.

This flying machine will help farmers water their tomatoes inside polytunnels. It's small, so it can fly into the polytunnels. It can carry the water and drop the water onto the tomatoes.

Get talking

Finding out about an exhibition

1 Choose a role card. Read and plan.

Student A

You want to see an exhibition at a museum.

You are making a phone call to find out about the following:

- if the exhibition is still on
- the opening times
- how much the ticket is
- how to get there by public transport from the railway station
- if there is a restaurant there

Student B

You work for the museum.

Someone is going to phone you to ask you some questions about an exhibition. Tell them:

- if the exhibition is still on
- about opening times
- about the price of tickets
- if there are long queues
- how to get there from the railway station
- if there is a restaurant at the museum

2 Act out your dialogue.

Student A

Is this the National Museum?
Is the exhibition … ?
What are the … ?
How much are … ?
Could you please tell me how to … ?
Is there a … ?

Student B

The exhibition …
We are open from …
The price of …
It might be a good idea to book …
There are …
Take bus number …
Yes, we've got …

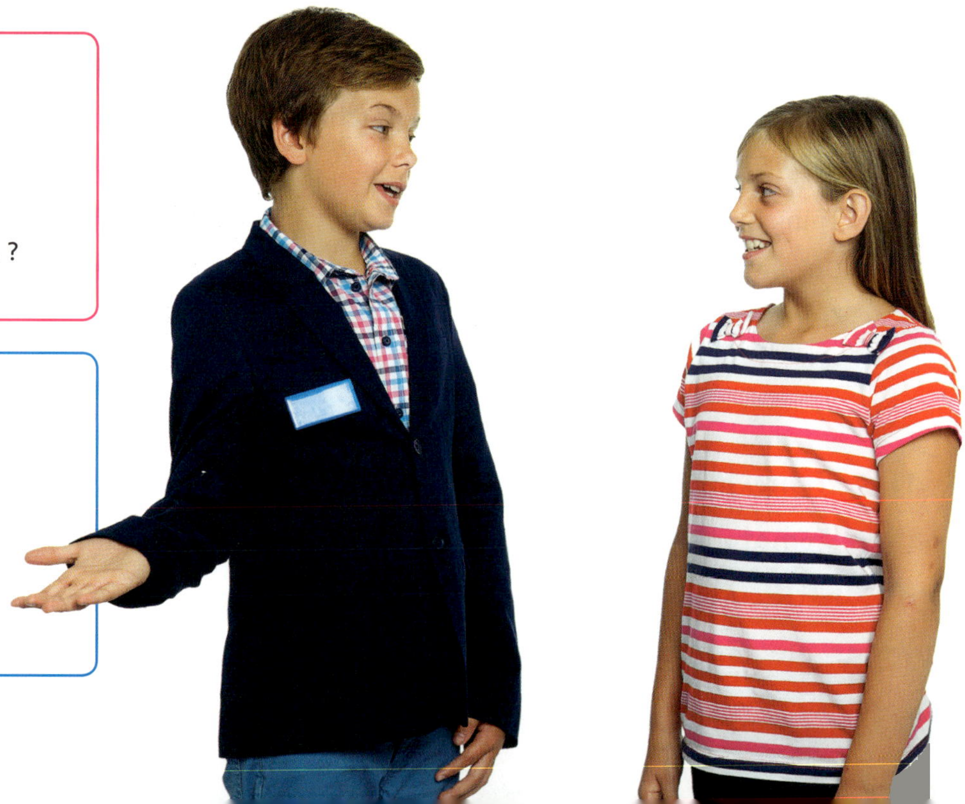

An advertisement

1 **Read this advertisement for a robot and answer the questions below.**

BUY ROBOLIX3000

– it'll be your **best friend for years** because it's the **most exciting robot in the universe.**

It'll make you happy on sad days and it'll help you if you are in trouble.

If you're bored, the robot will start playing the drums.

If you're hot, it'll bring you a glass of orange juice.

If you're hungry, it'll make you some sandwiches.

If you want to go for a walk and it starts raining, it'll bring an umbrella for you.

If you say 'Good night!', it'll start singing a beautiful song to help you sleep.

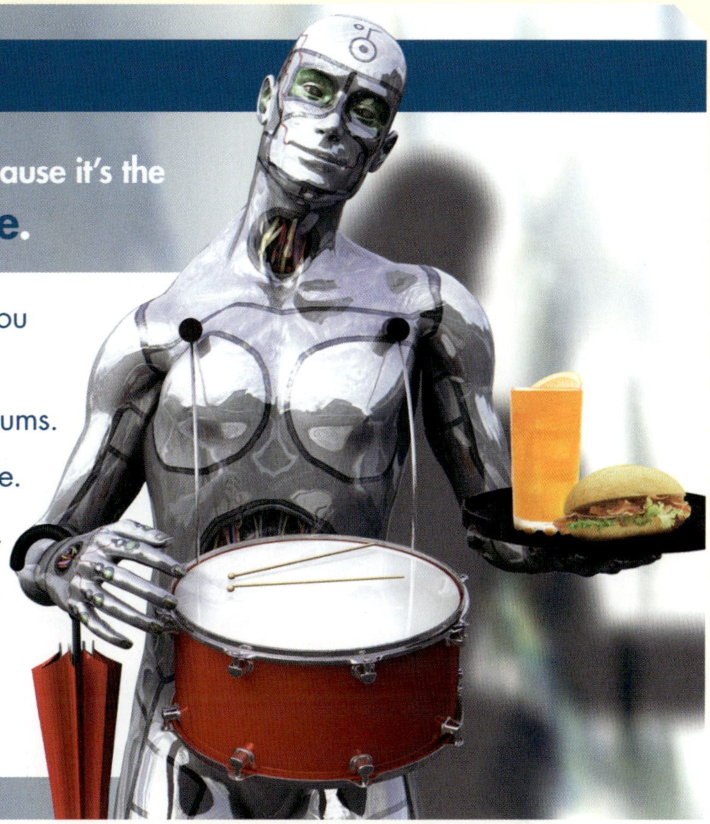

1 Why will ROBOLIX3000 be your best friend for years?
2 What will it do for you on sad days?
3 What will it do if you are in trouble?
4 What will happen if it starts raining?

ROBOLIX3000 will …

Writing tip

Before you start writing, think and make notes about your ideas.

2 **Imagine you are a scientist and are going to build a fancy robot. Write an advertisement for your robot.**

1 Write down all the things your robot will do to help:

* feel tired – make coffee
* are bored – play the saxophone
* go on holiday – take photos

2 Write an advertisement for your robot, so lots of people will buy it.

9 Mystery at sea

In the 19th century, the seas were full of ships like the one in the picture. People used them for transporting goods around the world. The journeys were often long and very dangerous. Ships spent many months at sea.

1 106 **Listen and say the words. Check with your partner.**

1 sail
2 sailor
3 captain
4 barometer
5 mast
6 rat
7 lifeboat
8 porthole
9 cabin

BIG QUESTION What do we know about the sea?

2 107 **Read, listen and complete the sentences.**

1 The ship is much ______________ than the *Titanic*.
2 The ship's ______________ is standing near the ______________.
3 Phoebe thinks they should ______________ for a while.
4 The ship's name is on the wall of the ______________ next to the ______________.

3 **Choose a word. Describe it for your partner to guess.**

You use it to check the weather.

Ah, I know, it's a barometer!

1 **Read Paul's webpage. Tick ✓ the flags of the places his uncle has visited.**

My uncle is a sailor and he's always travelling. So far, he's visited more than 105 countries, but he wants to visit every country in the world. There are 195 countries, so he's still got another 90 to go to. I think he's crazy.

He's already visited the USA and Mexico, but he hasn't visited Canada yet. He's been to South America, where he's visited Brazil and Chile. He hasn't visited Argentina yet.

He's been to Europe and visited Spain and the UK, but he hasn't visited Turkey yet. He's visited China and India, but he hasn't visited Australia yet. My uncle is already 75. I don't think he'll do it!

2 **Add *yet* and *already* to each sentence and say.**

1 My uncle's visited Mexico, but he hasn't visited Canada.

2 My uncle hasn't been to Turkey, but he's been to the UK.

3 108 **Watch, listen and say.**

Language focus

I'**ve already seen** a snake.
But I **haven't seen** a hippo **yet**.

He'**s already seen** a bat.
But he **hasn't seen** a zebra **yet**.

4 **Play the coin-tossing game.**

I've already done my …

I haven't done my …

1 109 Listen and write the rhyming words. Then sing the song.

swim side me sail ride see whale sea me in

Grandma and I one sunny day,
Went off for a nice boat **(1)** ____________,
When suddenly I turned around
She wasn't by my **(2)** ____________.

Captain drop the anchor,
Make your men jump **(3)** ____________,
My grandma's fallen in the sea,
I don't think she can **(4)** ____________!

I ran up to the telescope,
To see what I could **(5)** ____________.
I rubbed my eyes and looked again,
At the beast in front of **(6)** ____________.

Captain drop the anchor,
Captain drop the **(7)** ____________,
My grandma's fallen in the sea,
I think she's in a **(8)** ____________!

The captain dropped the anchor down,
His men jumped in the **(9)** ____________.
When suddenly I turned around,
My gran was next to **(10)** ____________!

'What's all the fuss about?'

All about music: Sea Shanties

Sea shanties were songs that sailors used to sing on their ships many years ago. Their work was often very hard and boring. The sailors were often at sea for many months at a time and the songs helped the days go quicker. Sea shanties are often played on accordions and tin whistles.

What I think about this song

It's great. It's OK. I don't really like it.

Phonics

2 111 Listen and say the dialogue.

Cookie You shouldn't put so much sugar in the pudding, Woody!

Woody But look, Cookie. The cookbook says, 'Six cupfuls'.

1 112 **Listen. Complete the dialogues with the words from the box. Match the dialogues to the pictures.**

parrot	dishes	kitchen	cabin	bath	soup	dinner

1 **Captain** Have you finished cleaning my ___________ yet?
Sailor Well, I've already swept it, but …
Captain But what?
Sailor … I haven't washed the floor yet.

2 **Captain** Have you finished making ___________ yet?
Sailor Well, I've already made the ___________ , but …
Captain But what?
Sailor … I haven't made the main course yet.

3 **Captain** Have you finished looking after my ___________ yet?
Sailor Well, I've already given him a ___________ , but …
Captain But what?
Sailor … I haven't fed him yet.

4 **Captain** Have you finished tidying the ___________ yet?
Sailor Well, I've already washed the ___________ , but …
Captain But what?
Sailor … I haven't cleaned the windows yet.

2 113 **Watch, listen and say.**

Language focus

Have you **put on** your boots **yet**?
My boots? No, I **haven't**. I **haven't done** that **yet**.
Have you **packed** your bag **yet**?
My bag? No, I **haven't**. I **haven't done** that **yet**.

3 **Play the housework game. Find out what your partner has or hasn't done this week.**

- do homework ☐
- walk dog ☐
- tidy bedroom ☐
- feed cat ☐
- do shopping ☐
- wash dishes ☐
- make breakfast ☐

Have you … yet?

Yes, I have. / No, I haven't.

The *Mary Celeste*

1 **Go through the story quickly and find answers to the questions.**

1 Why were the children hiding?

2 Why did one of the sailors know where the children were hiding?

2 114 **Read and listen to the story to check your answers.**

The children hid in a lifeboat and watched the sailors working. They didn't seem very friendly. Two of them came and stood by the lifeboat. 'I'm worried,' one of them said. 'The captain's nervous. He's already shouted at me three times today …' 'Atishoo!' sneezed Patrick. 'Whoops! I'm sorry!'

The sailors heard the noise and looked in the lifeboat. They found the children and took them to the captain. 'Look what we found!' one of them said. 'Lock them in my cabin,' said the captain. He looked worried. 'I'll talk to them later.'

The children looked around the cabin. The door would not open. 'Now, what?' Alex asked. 'We'll have to wait and see what the captain says,' said Patrick. Phoebe picked up a book from the table. 'Hey, listen guys. It's the captain's diary!' She read out, 'Things are strange. There is something wrong with this ship. I have a strong feeling that something bad is going to happen. 'Quick!' Patrick interrupted. 'Come and look out of the porthole!'

'Look at all those lights. It's our gate!' shouted Alex. 'We've got to go! But those lights are green,' said Phoebe. 'Our gate's yellow! That's very strange!'

'We've got to get out of here,' said Patrick. 'Let's break the door down.' The children picked up the table and banged it against the door. It opened and they walked out. There were green gates glowing all over the ship. The children were amazed. 'Look, there's a sailor. He's walking through one of the green gates!' shouted Alex. The sailor walked through the gate, and a second later he was gone. Everything was silent. There was no-one left!

'Now I remember,' said Alex. 'The *Mary Celeste* was the ship that they found with no-one on it. No-one knew what happened.' 'Now we know, but nobody would believe us,' said Phoebe. 'Look!' shouted Patrick. 'There's a yellow light. That's our gate. Come on!' The children stepped into the yellow gate. They were gone in a flash … and landed in their school playground with a thump.

'I don't believe it!' said Phoebe. 'We're home. Look there are Sam and Rob.' The Time Travellers ran over to their friends. 'Hey, guys!' said Patrick. 'You'll never guess what just happened. We had an incredible journey. That explosion in the Science lesson created a time tunnel… .' 'Very funny! We haven't had Science yet. It's this afternoon!' Sam laughed. 'Come on, lunch is nearly over and I want to play football.' The three friends looked at each other. Were they really back at the right time or was something wrong?

3 **Match the sentence halves to make the summary.**

1 The children hide in
2 The sailors talk about
3 The sailors lock the children in
4 Phoebe finds a diary on
5 Patrick looks out of
6 The children see lots of
7 The children use the table to break
8 The children arrive in

a the captain.
b the table.
c green lights.
d the door.
e the playground.
f the cabin.
g the porthole.
h a lifeboat.

4 **Read and add another answer for each question. Then choose the best answer.**

1 Why was the captain worried?
a The ship was going the wrong way. b His sailors were all aliens.
c ______________________________

2 Where did the sailors go?
a into a UFO b to another time
c ______________________________

3 What might be wrong back at school?
a It's not really their school. b Their friends don't believe their story.
c ______________________________

1 **Read the magazine article and match the questions from the box with the answers.**

So what's the truth?	Where is it?
What is it?	What has happened there?

It's a weird world:

THE BERMUDA TRIANGLE

1 ______________________

The Bermuda Triangle is an area at sea where many ships and planes have mysteriously disappeared. Nobody knows where they went.

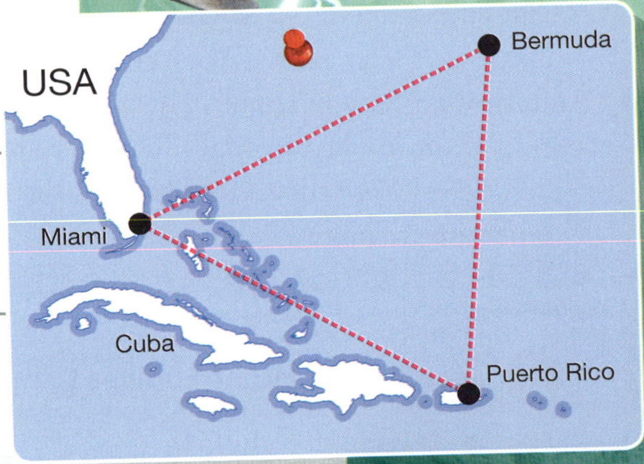

2 ______________________

The Bermuda Triangle is in the Atlantic Ocean. The corners of the 'triangle' are Miami, Bermuda and Puerto Rico.

3 ______________________

Here are two of the famous disappearances:

- In 1918, a ship called the US Cyclops disappeared in the area. None of the 306 people on the ship were ever seen again.
- In 1945, a group of fighter planes disappeared while they were flying over the area. The next day, another plane went to look for the missing fighters. This plane also disappeared.

4 ______________________

Some people say that there is nothing mysterious about the area. There are a lot of ships in this area, so it's not surprising that sometimes ships go missing. They also say that the bad weather in the area causes a lot of problems.

Other people think the area is more mysterious. Some people believe that aliens have taken the ships. Other people that a giant whirlpool pulls ships and planes under the sea.

WHAT DO YOU THINK?

2 **Read again and correct the sentences.**

1 The Bermuda Triangle is in the Pacific Ocean.
2 Only ships disappear in the area.
3 The US Cyclops was a plane.
4 In 1945, a plane disappeared in the area.
5 Not many ships sail in the area.
6 The weather is always good in the area.

3 **What do you think? Discuss in pairs then share your opinion with the class.**

I think the Bermuda Triangle is …

Maybe it is …

Do you really think so?

That's a good idea.

1 115 **Listen to the radio show *World of Mysteries*. Write the names of the creatures under the pictures.**

the Loch Ness Monster
the Kraken a siren

______ ______ ______

2 116 **Listen again and write the names of the creatures next to the sentences.**

1 They sang beautifully. ______
2 It pulled ships under the sea. ______
3 It doesn't live in the sea. ______
4 Everyone wants a photo of this. ______
5 They made ships crash into rocks. ______

3 **Imagine a monster that lives in the sea or a lake. Draw and write about your monster.**

1 Think about the monster you want to write about and draw. Make notes about:
- adjectives that describe it
- its name
- where it lives and what it does.

2 Read your notes to a partner. Make suggestions to help each other.
3 Draw your monster and write a paragraph about it.
4 Present your monster to your classmates. Which monster is the scariest, which is most beautiful and which is most imaginative?

This is a Trifish. It has three heads and lots of teeth. It lives in ponds in the middle of forests. Don't put your toes in the water – it likes to bite feet!

Marine animals

What kinds of marine animals are there?

1 Read and write the missing information.

They give milk to their babies. They only live in water. They live on land and water.

Super fact!

Most crocodiles live in rivers, but some crocodiles live in the sea. We call them *saltwater crocodiles*.

Warm-blooded animals can stay hot when their environment is cold. **Cold-blooded** animals are hot when their environment is hot and cold when their environment is cold.

Mammals

- ______________________
- They are warm-blooded.
- They don't lay eggs.

sea otters

Reptiles

- They are cold-blooded.
- They can't breathe underwater.
- ______________________

Fish

- They can breathe underwater.
- They are cold-blooded.
- ______________________

clown fish

saltwater crocodile

2 Work in pairs. Is it a fish, mammal or reptile?

Number one is a …

3 Read about camouflage. Can you see the fish in the picture?

Many marine animals use **camouflage** to hide from other animals. Some fish have colours and patterns that look like sea plants. Sea turtles have colours and patterns on their shells that look like rocks. Dolphins and whales often have dark backs so they are camouflaged at the top of the water.

4 Read the fact files. Then write *turtle* or *orca*.

Marine animal: Green sea turtle
Type of animal: Reptile
Lives for: Up to 100 years.
How fast? They can swim from 3 to 35 kilometres an hour.
Eats: Sea plants, and grasses (they're herbivores).
Camouflage: Their shells can look like the sea and sand so they are camouflaged when they are in the sea or on the beach.
Special features: They lay eggs in the sand on beaches.

Marine animal: Orca
Type of animal: Mammal
Lives for: Up to 80 years.
How fast? They can swim 46 kilometres an hour.
Eats: Fish, seals, penguins, sharks, sea turtles, blue whales (they're carnivores).
Camouflage: When they swim quickly, their black and white bodies can camouflage them from fish, seals and penguins.
Special features: They work together in a family to find food.

Which animal:

1 is the fastest? __________
2 lives the longest? __________
3 is cold-blooded? __________
4 eats other animals? __________
5 lays eggs? __________

5 Project **Make a fact file about a marine animal.**

- Choose an animal and find out:
  - Is it a reptile, a fish or a mammal?
  - How long does it live for?
  - Is it fast?
  - What does it eat?
  - Does it use camouflage?
  - What other special features does it have?
- Draw the animal in the sea or find images of it.
- Make your fact file.

Time to present

Small-group talk

1 117 **Listen to Ruby, Mike and Sue talking about UFOs. Put these key words in the order you hear them.**

- [ ] little green men
- [ ] farmer
- [ ] UFO
- [ ] scientist

2 118 **Listen again and answer the questions.**

1 What does Ruby talk about?
2 What story does Mike tell?
3 What does Sue say?

Ruby talks about …

3 **Give a small-group talk.**

Find out about it

- Work in groups of three. Choose an unexplained mystery and find out more about it.
- Possible topics are: Bigfoot, the Yeti …
- Use books and magazines.
- Talk to your family and to friends.
- Go online and see what you can find on the Internet.
- In your group, decide what each of you is going to talk about.

Prepare it

- Each of you tries to find out some important facts about the mystery. Take notes. Compare your notes. Put them in order.
- Find pictures and print them out. Make sure the pictures or photos are big enough for your classmates to see from a distance.
- Decide what each of you is going to say and write your part of the talk. Then show it to your teacher to help you with the language.
- Correct the text if necessary. Read it often enough so that you know what you will say.
- Practise it as a group. Each of you should know when the other one stops so you know when to start. Decide when to show the pictures.

Present it

- Tell your classmates about your topic and present the pictures.
- You should talk for about a minute, but do not just read your text.
- Make sure that all your classmates can see the pictures.

Presenting tip

When you practise, check if one of you says 'um' or 'ah' a lot. If you do, try not to. Your classmates may think that you have not prepared well if there are lots of 'ums' and 'ahs'.

Think and write

A summary

1 **Read the summary of the first four episodes of the Time Travellers' story and complete with the words from the box. Use each word twice.**

and so but because

Alex, Phoebe and Patrick are friends. One day, they have an accident in the school Science lab (1) __________ they create a gateway to different times and places. First, they visit ancient Pompeii. Phoebe sees smoke coming from the volcano and wants to warn the people (2) __________ the children go to the city. However, the volcano erupts and it's too late for the people (3) __________ the children escape when the gateway appears.

Next, the children find themselves in the middle of the jungle. Phoebe thinks they are in South America (4) __________ she can see a jaguar. The children walk through the jungle (5) __________ they meet some people. Alex gives them a penknife as a present. Then they see the gateway at the top of a waterfall (6) __________ they climb up it and jump through it.

Next, the children are in 1950s America watching Elvis on stage. After the show, they talk to him. He is afraid to leave (7) __________ there are lots of fans waiting for him. The children think of a plan to help him escape. The children want to stay with Elvis (8) __________ they know they have to go through the gateway again. They are trying to get home.

2 **Read the summary of the next three episodes. Write it again and use *and, so, but* or *because* to put together the sentence pairs that are marked in colour.**

1 The children are now in the future in a restaurant at the edge of the universe. They find out it is Phoebe's birthday. They decide to celebrate. They have an amazing meal with lots of wonderful food and a birthday cake. The waiter tells them that the meal costs 60,000 goldstars. The children don't have any money. The waiter takes them to the kitchen to wash up. They are saved because the gateway appears.

2 The children arrive in the Wild West. A bank robbery is taking place. They talk to the sheriff. He doesn't do anything. He is scared of the robbers. Alex has a plan. He ties a rope around the robbers' horses' legs. The robbers fall off their horses. The sheriff arrests them. The kids disappear through the gateway.

3 The next place they arrive in is Istanbul. They decide to go sightseeing, but Phoebe misses the train. She is lost. The boys try to find her. A Turkish boy helps them. Finally, they find Phoebe and they say goodbye to their new friend as they walk through the gateway to a new adventure.

Writing tip

When you write a summary, only focus on the most important information. When you have finished, read your text again. Imagine somebody who has not read the original story is reading it. Would they understand it?

3 **Write a summary of the final three episodes of the Time Travellers' story. Use *and, so, but* and *because* to put sentences together.**

Language focus The Science lesson

Past simple revision

I/He/She **was** at a birthday party.
It **was** very cold.
We/You/They **were** at the zoo.
I/You/He/She/It/We/You/They **loved** the food.
I/You/He/She/It/We/You/They **didn't like** the music.

I/He/She **wasn't** late.
It **wasn't** sunny.
We/You/They **weren't** at the party.

1 **Complete the sentences with the verbs in brackets.**

1 Yesterday, I ________________ a lot of work to do. (have)
2 I ________________ up very early. (get)
3 I ________________ all day. (study)
4 In the evening, I ________________ my dad in the kitchen. (help)
5 He ________________ very happy about that. (be)
6 In the evening, I ________________ TV. I ________________ too tired. (not watch / be)

Past simple questions revision

Was I too loud this morning?
Was he angry?
Was she happy?
Were you at home?
Were they at the shops?

Did I **wake** you up?
Why did you **phone** me?
Did he **help** you?
How did she **go** to school?
Did it **win**?
Did we **wake** you up?
What did they **say**?

2 **Choose the correct words.**

1 What did she **study/studied**?
2 **Was/Were** your sister on holiday?
3 **Was/Were** they very hungry?
4 **Did/Do** you visit your grandfather yesterday?
5 **How did/How do** your exam go?
6 Why **was/were** you late this morning?

1 Disaster!

Past continuous revision

What **were** you **doing** when the fire started? I **was playing** the guitar You **were reading** a book He **was playing** the piano She **was cooking** It **was raining** We/You/They **were dancing**	when the fire started.

1 Choose the correct words.

1 I **was/were** eating when the phone rang.
2 When the boat arrived, we **was/were** buying the tickets.
3 They **was/were** cooking when the lights went off.
4 You were sleeping when the film **started / was starting.**
5 When the phone rang, she **worked / was working** in the garden.

Two simultaneous actions with *while*

While I **was talking** on the phone, **While** you **were playing** football, **While** he/she **was repairing** the car, **While** it **was sunny**, **While** we **were swimming** in the pool, **While** they **were having** a barbecue,	the tortoise **was eating** the flowers.

2 Complete the sentences with the verbs in brackets.

1 While we ________________ TV, they were lying in the sun. (watch)
2 While he ________________ to his neighbour, the dog was barking loudly. (talk)
3 They were playing football while their friends ________________ to music. (listen)
4 I ________________ Dad while you were playing. (help)
5 You were walking the dog while I ________________ for my test. (study)

2 In the rainforest

Numbers 100–1,000,000

100 – **one hundred**	500 – **five hundred**
1,000 – **a thousand**	5,000 – **five thousand**
10,000 – **ten thousand**	30,000 – **thirty thousand**
100,000 – **one hundred thousand**	600,000 – **six hundred thousand**
1,000,000 – **one million**	2,000,000 – **two million**

1 Write the numbers or the words.

1 13,000	–	________
2 ________	–	twelve million
3 4,000	–	________
4 900,000	–	________
5 ________	–	seventy thousand

Have to / Had to revision

I/You **have to** eat healthily.
I/You **had to** train hard.
You **don't have to** do a lot of weightlifting.
Do I have to smile?

2 Make sentences and questions.

1 to/nine/have/You/bed/go/before/to/. ________
2 before/get/You/have/don't/to/up/eight/. ________
3 homework/had/of/do/lot/a/We/to/. ________
4 I/Do/to/have/you/phone/? ________
5 we/to/Do/bring/have/food/any/? ________
6 to/You/had/us/come/with/. ________

3 The rock 'n' roll show

Going to revision

I'**m going to** be late!	It'**s not going to** rain.
Are you **going to** play in our team?	We'**re going to** help you.
He'**s going to** write me an email.	You'**re not going to** win the match.
She'**s going to** meet her friends tomorrow.	They'**re going to** record a new song.

1 **Make sentences.**

1 come/not/to/today/They're/school/to/going/.

____

2 going/read/to/book/over/this/I'm/the/weekend/.

____

3 not/pizza/going/She's/make/to/.

____

4 going/They're/table/to/tennis/play/.

____

5 watch/not/going/the/to/match/We're/.

____

Time: *past* and *to* the hour

It's **twenty past** five.

It's **ten past** twelve.

It's **twenty to** twelve.

It's **ten to** twelve.

2 **Complete the sentences.**

1 It's ______________________.

2 It's ______________________.

3 It's ______________________.

4 It's ______________________.

1 

2 

3 

4 

4 Space restaurant

Ordinal numbers

the **1st (first)** of January
the **2nd (second)** of January
the **3rd (third)** of January
the **4th (fourth)** of January
the **5th (fifth)** of January

1 Complete the sentences with the dates in brackets.

1 His birthday's on the 17th (seventeenth) of May (17 May)
2 He's going to leave on the ________________. (1 December)
3 It's on ________________. (31 January)
4 His holiday starts on ________________. (13 February)
5 She's arriving on ________________. (2 October)

Zero conditional

If you **put** a candle near the oven, it **melts**.
If it **rains**, the grass **gets** wet.
If you **stay** in the sun for too long, you **get** sunburned.

2 Complete the sentences with the verbs in brackets.

1 If flowers ________________ water, they die. (not get)
2 If you heat water to 100 degrees, it ________________. (boil)
3 If you put salt on ice, it ________________. (melt)
4 If a flame ________________ air, it doesn't burn. (not get)
5 If a car ________________ of petrol, it stops. (run out)

5 The Wild West

Be made of … / Be used for …

This elephant **is made of** glass.
My jeans **are made of** cotton.
This wood**'s used for** making furniture.
These books **are used for** teaching French.

1 Make sentences.

1 pencil case/The/made/cotton/of/is/. ______
2 are/made/My/leather/of/cow/shoes/. ______
3 blankets/for/These/covering/paintings/used/are/the/. ______
4 notebooks/are/for/These/drawing/used/pictures/. ______
5 used/Gold/is/jewellery/for/making/. ______

Possessive apostrophes

The **pilot's** uniform is dark blue.
The **pilots'** sunglasses look cool.
The **tortoise's** shoes are a little too big.
My **sisters'** computers are new.
My **dad's** car is quite old.
My **parents'** books are in our living room

2 Match the pictures with the sentences. Write numbers.

1 The girls' jeans are green.
2 The teacher's glasses are red.
3 The boy's jeans are grey.
4 The teachers' glasses are red.
5 The boys' jeans are grey.
6 The girl's jeans are green.

6 In Istanbul

Should / Shouldn't

You **should** listen carefully to your teacher.
You **shouldn't** make so much noise in class.

1 Choose the correct words.

1 It's hot. You **should/shouldn't** wear your coat.
2 You have found a golden ring. You **should/shouldn't** report your find.
3 Your little brother has built a sandcastle. You **should**/**shouldn't** destroy it.
4 There's a great film on tonight. You **should/shouldn't** come to the cinema with us.
5 There are snakes around. You **should/shouldn't** be careful.

Could I … ? / Do you mind if I … ?

Could you tell me what bus goes to the main square? Of course.
Could I try on this hat, please?
Do you mind if I look at the cameras? Not at all.

2 Make questions.

1 me/you/Could/show/way/the/to/stadium/the/?

____

2 you/Do/use/mind/I/your/mobile/if/phone/?

____

3 you/station/tell/where/me/the/is/Could/?

____

4 I/talk/Could/for/five/to/minutes/you/?

____

5 I/have/tea/Could/cup/another/of/please/?

____

6 you/Do/if/tomorrow/I/come/mind/back/?

____

7 The story teller

Will for offers and promises

A We need some games for the party. **B** **I'll ask** my mum to help us.
A It's so cold in here. **B** **I'll shut** the window.
A I've got a cold. **B** **I'll give** you some medication.

1 **Complete the sentences with the verbs in brackets.**

1 There are no sandwiches left. I ________________ some more. (make)
2 I'm thirsty. I ________________ you some orange juice. (get)
3 There's someone at the door. I ________________ a look. (have)
4 There's been an accident. I ________________ the police. (phone)
5 Peter's still sleeping. I ________________ him up. (wake)

Present perfect with *just*

I**'ve just spoken** to her. (= have just spoken)
You**'ve just broken** my pen. (= have just broken)
Tom**'s just left** for school. (= has just left)
Karen**'s just phoned**.
The tortoise **has just discovered** a new friend.
We**'ve just seen** her.
They**'ve just heard** the good news.

2 **Complete the sentences with the verbs in brackets. Use *just* and the present perfect.**

1 Tom's very happy. He ______________________ a lovely present. (get)
2 Ouch! I ______________________ my knee. (hurt)
3 I'm still tired. I ______________________ up. (get)
4 Tom and Peter are coming tomorrow!
They ______________________ . (phone)
5 Look! I ______________________ a beautiful feather. (find)
6 We're not hungry. We ______________________ lunch. (have)

8 Museum of the future

First conditional

If it **rains**, **I'll** take my umbrella.
If you'**re** cold, **I'll** give you my pullover.
If they'**re** late, there **won't** be any food for them.

1 **Complete the sentences with the verbs in brackets.**

1 If you like fruit, I ________________ you some mangos. (get)
2 If you send me an email, I ________________ to bring your books. (not forget)
3 If the sun ________________, we'll go swimming. (shine)
4 If you aren't careful, you ________________ your leg. (break)
5 If our teacher ________________ that, he won't be happy. (hear)

What if … ?

A Let's go swimming.
B But **what if** it rains?
A Then we'll go home again.

A Let's bake a cake for our friends.
B But **what if** it doesn't taste good?
A Then we'll buy one!

2 **Make sentences and questions.**

1 **A** eat/Let's/apples/these/.

____

B what/are/if/they/not/good/But/?

____

A we'll/Then/some/eat/bananas/.

____

2 **A** buy/that/Let's/car/.

____

B if/But/what/it's/expensive/too/?

____

A Then/buy/a/we'll/motorbike/.

____

9 Mystery at sea

Present perfect with *already* and *yet*

I**'ve already been** to New York.
You**'ve already told** me that.
He**'s already had** lunch.
She**'s already heard** this song.
It**'s already been** eaten.
We**'ve already tried** this food.
They**'ve already been** here.
I/You/We/They **haven't seen** this yet.
He/She **hasn't done** her homework yet.

1 **Make sentences.**

1 hasn't/She/to/London/been/yet/. ______
2 already/the/They've/money/found/. ______
3 told/I/you/haven't/yet/. ______
4 already/all/read/the/We've/books/. ______
5 yet/haven't/shopping/done/You/the/. ______

Have you … yet?

A **Have** you **phoned** your brother **yet**?
B Yes, **I've already** done it.
A **Have** you **phoned** your sister **yet**?
B No, **I haven't done** it **yet**.
A **Have** you **cooked** the spaghetti **yet**?
B Yes, **I've already** done it.

2 **Complete the sentences with the verbs in brackets.**

1 **A** Have you ______ your bike yet? (clean)
B Yes, ______.
2 **A** Have you ______ your dinner yet? (eat)
B No, ______.
3 **A** Have you ______ your homework yet? (do)
B Yes, ______.
4 **A** Have you ______ your room yet? (tidy)
B No, ______.